WAITING FOR THE SAVIOR

THE GENEALOGY OF JESUS
AND THE HOPE OF CHRISTMAS

THE DAILY GRACE CO.

STUDY SUGGESTIONS

We believe that the Bible is true, trustworthy, and timeless and that it is vitally important for all believers. These study suggestions are intended to help you more effectively study Scripture as you seek to know and love God through His Word.

SUGGESTED STUDY TOOLS

◯ A Bible

◯ A double-spaced, printed copy of the Scripture passages that this study covers. You can use a website like *www.biblegateway.com* to copy the text of a passage and print out a double-spaced copy to be able to mark on easily.

◯ A journal to write notes or prayers

◯ Pens, colored pencils, and highlighters

◯ A dictionary to look up unfamiliar words

HOW TO USE THIS STUDY

Begin your study time in prayer. Ask God to reveal Himself to you, to help you understand what you are reading, and to transform you with His Word (Psalm 119:18).

Before you read what is written in each day of the study itself, read the assigned passages of Scripture for that day. Use your double-spaced copy to circle, underline, highlight, draw arrows, and mark in any way you would like to help you dig deeper as you work through a passage.

Read the daily written content provided for the current study day.

Answer the questions that appear at the end of each study day.

The inductive method provides tools for deeper and more intentional Bible study. To study a book of the Bible inductively, work through the steps below after reading background information on the book.

1   ## OBSERVATION & COMPREHENSION
Key question: What does the text say?

After reading the book of the Bible in its entirety at least once, begin working with smaller portions of the book. Read a passage of Scripture repetitively, and then mark the following items in the text:

- Key or repeated words and ideas
- Key themes
- Transition words *(Ex: therefore, but, because, if/then, likewise, etc.)*
- Lists
- Comparisons & Contrasts
- Commands
- Unfamiliar words (look these up in a dictionary)
- Questions you have about the text

2   ## INTERPRETATION
Key question: What does the text mean?

Once you have annotated the text, work through the following steps to help you interpret its meaning:

- Read the passage in other versions for a better understanding of the text.
- Read cross-references to help interpret Scripture with Scripture.
- Paraphrase or summarize the passage to check for understanding.
- Identify how the text reflects the metanarrative of Scripture, which is the story of creation, fall, redemption, and restoration.
- Read trustworthy commentaries if you need further insight into the meaning of the passage.

3

APPLICATION
Key Question: How should the truth of this passage change me?

Bible study is not merely an intellectual pursuit. The truths about God, ourselves, and the gospel that we discover in Scripture should produce transformation in our hearts and lives. Answer the following questions as you consider what you have learned in your study:

- What attributes of God's character are revealed in the passage?

    Consider places where the text directly states the character of God, as well as how His character is revealed through His words and actions.

- What do I learn about myself in light of who God is?

    Consider how you fall short of God's character, how the text reveals your sin nature, and what it says about your new identity in Christ.

- How should this truth change me?

    A passage of Scripture may contain direct commands telling us what to do or warnings about sins to avoid in order to help us grow in holiness. Other times our application flows out of seeing ourselves in light of God's character. As we pray and reflect on how God is calling us to change in light of His Word, we should be asking questions like, "How should I pray for God to change my heart?" and "What practical steps can I take toward cultivating habits of holiness?"

ATTRIBUTES OF GOD

ETERNAL

God has no beginning and no end. He always was, always is, and always will be.

HAB. 1:12 / REV. 1:8 / IS. 41:4

FAITHFUL

God is incapable of anything but fidelity. He is loyally devoted to His plan and purpose.

2 TIM. 2:13 / DEUT. 7:9
HEB. 10:23

GLORIOUS

God is ultimately beautiful, deserving of all praise and honor.

REV. 19:1 / PS. 104:1
EX. 40:34-35

GOOD

God is pure; there is no defilement in Him. He is unable to sin, and all He does is good.

GEN. 1:31 / PS. 34:8 / PS. 107:1

GRACIOUS

God is kind, giving to us gifts and benefits which we do not deserve.

2 KINGS 13:23 / PS. 145:8
IS. 30:18

HOLY

God is undefiled and unable to be in the presence of defilement. He is sacred and set-apart.

REV. 4:8 / LEV. 19:2 / HAB. 1:13

IMMUTABLE

God does not change. He is the same yesterday, today, and tomorrow.

1 SAM. 15:29 / ROM. 11:29
JAMES 1:17

JEALOUS

God is desirous of receiving the praise and affection He rightly deserves.

EX. 20:5 / DEUT. 4:23-24
JOSH. 24:19

JUST

God governs in perfect justice. He acts in accordance with justice. In Him there is no wrongdoing or dishonesty.

IS. 61:8 / DEUT. 32:4 / PS. 146:7-9

LOVE

God is eternally, enduringly, steadfastly loving and affectionate. He does not forsake or betray His covenant love.

JN. 3:16 / EPH. 2:4-5 / 1 JN. 4:16

MERCIFUL

God is compassionate, withholding us from the wrath that we deserve.

TITUS 3:5 / PS. 25:10
LAM. 3:22-23

OMNIPOTENT

God is all-powerful; His strength is unlimited.

MAT. 19:26 / JOB 42:1-2
JER. 32:27

OMNIPRESENT

God is everywhere; His presence is near and permeating.

PROV. 15:3 / PS. 139:7-10
JER. 23:23-24

OMNISCIENT

God is all-knowing; there is nothing unknown to Him.

PS. 147:4 / I JN. 3:20
HEB. 4:13

PATIENT

God is long-suffering and enduring. He gives ample opportunity for people to turn toward Him.

ROM. 2:4 / 2 PET. 3:9 / PS. 86:15

RIGHTEOUS

God is blameless and upright. There is no wrong found in Him.

PS. 119:137 / JER. 12:1
REV. 15:3

SOVEREIGN

God governs over all things; He is in complete control.

COL. 1:17 / PS. 24:1-2
1 CHRON. 29:11-12

TRUE

God is our measurement of what is fact. By Him are we able to discern true and false.

JN. 3:33 / ROM. 1:25 / JN. 14:6

WISE

God is infinitely knowledgeable and is judicious with His knowledge.

IS. 46:9-10 / IS. 55:9 / PROV. 3:19

Creation

In the beginning, God created the universe. He made the world and everything in it. He created humans in His own image to be His representatives on the earth.

Fall

The first humans, Adam and Eve, disobeyed God by eating from the fruit of the Tree of Knowledge of Good and Evil. Because of sin, the world was cursed. The punishment for sin is death, and because of Adam's original sin, all humans are sinful and condemned to death.

Redemption

God sent his Son to become a human and redeem His people. Jesus Christ lived a sinless life but died on the cross to pay the penalty for sin. He resurrected from the dead and ascended into heaven. All who put their faith in Jesus are saved from death and freely receive the gift of eternal life.

Restoration

One day, Jesus Christ will return again and restore all that sin destroyed. He will usher in a new heaven and new earth where all who trust in Him will live eternally with glorified bodies in the presence of God.

contents

hope

hope

hope

hope

hope

hope

01 / 01
CANDLE LIGHTING DAY

hope

THE FIRST CANDLE OF ADVENT REPRESENTS
THE HOPE THAT WE HAVE IN CHRIST.

PRAYER

Oh God of hope, as we begin this Advent season, we remember Christ and the hope that You secured for us. In Your coming as a baby, living a perfect life, and dying for our sins on the cross, You sealed our inheritance to live eternally with You. You have given us a hope that does not disappoint, for You promise that all who trust in You will be saved. You are the longing of our souls, our unwavering hope, and the One for whom we wait with patience. Even as Your Spirit dwells within us, we long to see You face to face. Help us wait patiently because we miss You. Open our eyes to see the hope that You have called us to and the all-sufficiency of Your love this Christmas season. Thank You, Lord.

this
hope

This hope will not disappoint us, because God's love has been poured out in our hearts through the Holy Spirit who was given to us.

ROMANS 5:5

We will see a
glimpse of the glory
of God's plan
for Christmas that
began even before the
universe was formed.

The Family Line of Jesus

Advent is a season of waiting and longing for the promised Savior. The word "advent" means "coming or arrival," and during the weeks leading up to Christmas, believers throughout the centuries and around the world have joined together to prepare their hearts for the coming of the long-expected Jesus Christ. As we set aside the next four weeks to intentionally cultivate our longing for the Savior and lean into waiting, we want to remember that the wait for Jesus was long. We wait twelve months, and more specifically four weeks, to celebrate the birth of Jesus on Christmas morning, but the people of God who lived before His coming waited thousands of years from the first promise of Jesus to His birth in Bethlehem. Generations and generations of those who waited and yearned for a savior are represented in the names of the genealogy of Jesus.

The New Testament begins in Matthew 1:1 with the words, "An account of the genealogy of Jesus Christ, the son of David, the son of Abraham." We might be tempted to read quickly through the list of names that follow, seeing them as a formality before the real content of the book of Matthew. We might think that this long list of names is a very unexciting way to start the Christmas story, but this sentiment fails to recognize the joy that results from understanding the rich history represented in the genealogy of Jesus. During this study, we will take a look at many of the stories of the people in Jesus's family tree. We will see a glimpse of the glory of God's plan for Christmas that began even before the universe was formed. Each person in the genealogy is a testament to God's goodness and grace. Every name proclaims the faithfulness of the Lord who is sovereign over every detail. Each new generation represents years of waiting through seasons of joy and suffering. Christmas is the answer to thousands of long years of waiting and longing for the Savior.

The genealogy in Matthew 1 begins with Abraham, but Jesus's family tree goes back to Adam and Eve. God created the first humans in His image to be His representatives on earth. In Genesis 3, Adam and Eve disobeyed God's command, and God pronounced the curse of sin on all creation. The punishment for sin is death, and the disobedience of Adam and Eve left them condemned. Because of the sin of Adam, all humans have inherited a sinful nature and are condemned to death. In God's incredible grace, even as He proclaimed the sorrow of the curse, He promised the hope of salvation. In Genesis 3:15, God gave the first, veiled gospel that would be progressively uncovered until it was fully revealed in Jesus Christ. To the serpent who deceived Eve, God said, "I will put hostility between you and the woman, and between your offspring and her offspring. He will strike your head, and you will strike his heel."

God promised that there would be an offspring of the woman who would be born to defeat Satan. Adam and Eve did not know it, but the promised offspring would be Jesus Christ. The serpent would wound, but he would not have victory over Christ. Jesus would endure the pain of the cross, but even His death would not be final. When Christ died on the cross, it seemed as if the devil had won and hope was lost, but even though Satan bruised the Savior's heel, the wounds left by the serpent would be the very thing that would crush him under the feet of Jesus. Christ is not defeated in His death but is victorious over the power of sin and death in His resurrection. The hope of Christmas is not just a baby born in a manger—it is the arrival of the awaited offspring who was born to die so that sinners could become children of God.

Adam and Eve hoped that their son would be the one to defeat the devil, but the sin of their offspring manifested openly when Cain murdered his brother, Abel. As the years passed, each new generation proved to be corrupted by sin, and no offspring was found who was worthy to save God's people. Still, God remained faithful to provide a savior. Year after year, God's promise of redemption passed from one generation to the next through a specific family line. There was nothing particularly impressive about this family that made them a desirable choice. In fact, the genealogy of Jesus is marked by sin and brokenness at every turn—a group of misfits and miscreants chosen by God's grace to be instruments of His perfect plan and recipients of His promise.

The waiting for that first Christmas was long. At times, it likely seemed as if God had forgotten His promises and turned His back on His people, but when the time was just right, the light of Christ tore through the darkness. Advent is a reminder that we too are in a season of waiting. Old Testament believers waited for the arrival of Jesus Christ, and we wait for Him to come again. As we look back at the faithfulness of God to send the promised offspring through seemingly impossible circumstances, our hearts are strengthened in confidence that Christ will come again. The hope, peace, joy, and love of Christ that we experience in part now, we will experience in full at His second advent.

BUT WHEN THE TIME WAS JUST RIGHT, THE LIGHT OF CHRIST TORE THROUGH THE DARKNESS.

WHY DO YOU THINK IT IS VALUABLE TO LOOK BACK AT THE FAMILY TREE OF JESUS AS WE PREPARE OUR HEARTS FOR CHRISTMAS?

READ GALATIANS 4:4-5. WHAT DOES THIS PASSAGE REVEAL ABOUT GOD'S TIMING IN SENDING JESUS? HOW DOES THAT ENCOURAGE YOU AS YOU WAIT FOR HIS SECOND COMING?

WRITE A PRAYER AS YOU ENTER INTO THE ADVENT SEASON. ASK GOD TO INCREASE YOUR LONGING FOR JESUS AND STRENGTHEN YOUR FAITH AS YOU SEE HIS CHARACTER.

Genealogy of Jesus

FROM MATTHEW 1

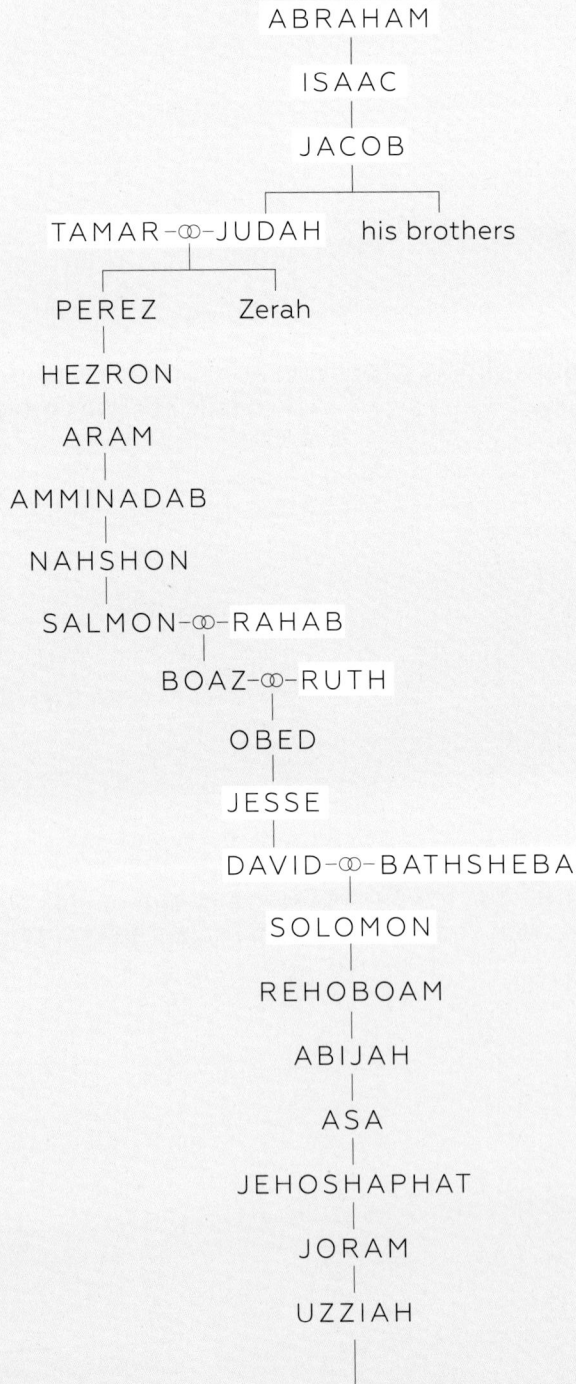

ABRAHAM

ISAAC

JACOB

TAMAR–∞–JUDAH   his brothers

PEREZ   Zerah

HEZRON

ARAM

AMMINADAB

NAHSHON

SALMON–∞–RAHAB

BOAZ–∞–RUTH

OBED

JESSE

DAVID–∞–BATHSHEBA

SOLOMON

REHOBOAM

ABIJAH

ASA

JEHOSHAPHAT

JORAM

UZZIAH

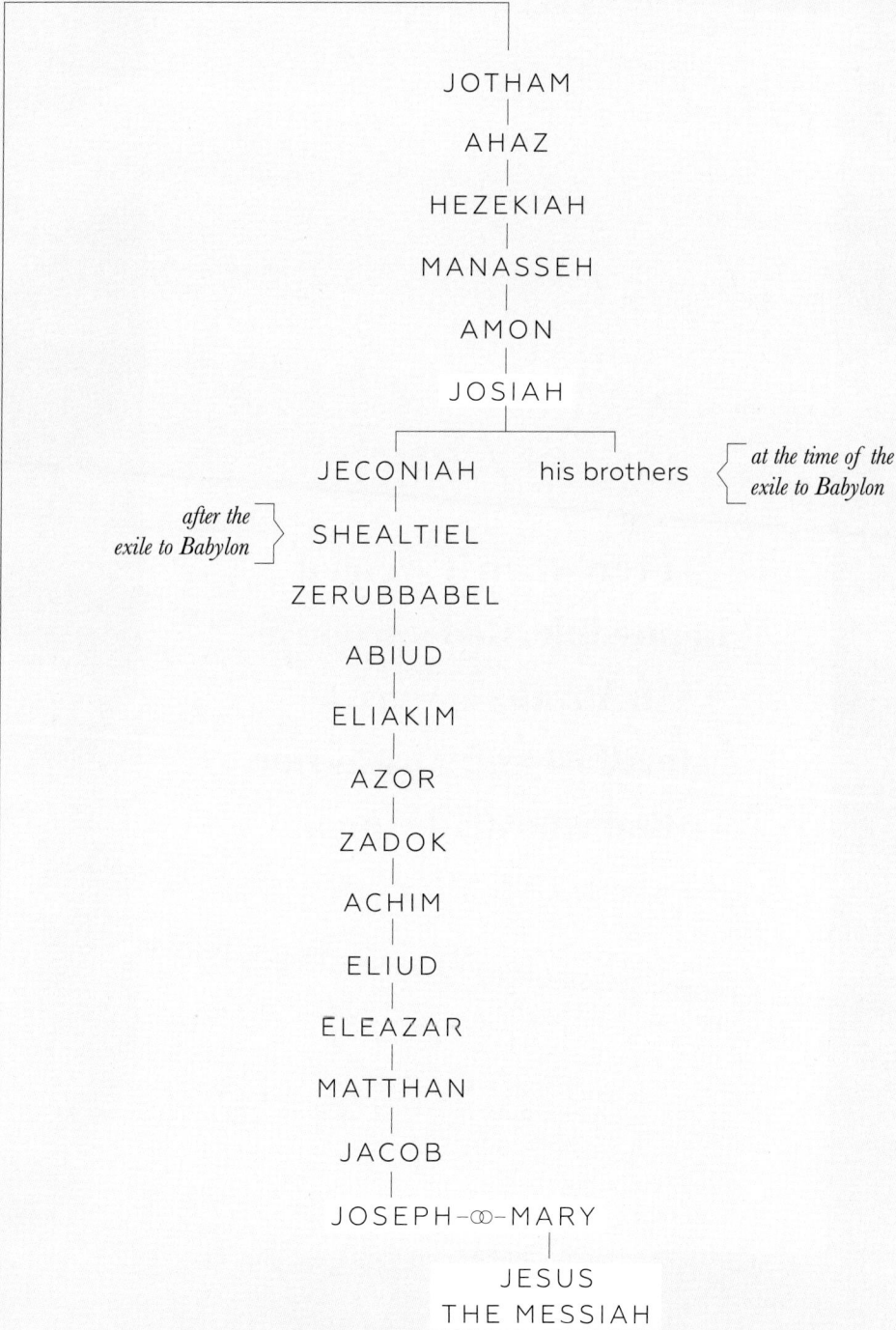

JOTHAM

AHAZ

HEZEKIAH

MANASSEH

AMON

JOSIAH

JECONIAH   his brothers   { *at the time of the*
                                      exile to Babylon

after the   SHEALTIEL
exile to Babylon

ZERUBBABEL

ABIUD

ELIAKIM

AZOR

ZADOK

ACHIM

ELIUD

ELEAZAR

MATTHAN

JACOB

JOSEPH—∞—MARY

JESUS
THE MESSIAH

01 / 03

Even when it seemed impossible, God's promises to Abraham were as steadfast and sure as the God who made them.

Abraham

The genealogy of Jesus begins with a reminder of an extraordinary promise. The first name listed in the genealogy is Abraham, an ordinary man whom God chose to use for an extraordinary purpose. Through Abraham's family line, God would bring about the Redeemer who would save His people from their sins.

Abraham seemed like an unlikely choice to be an instrument of God's plan. He came from a pagan family who worshiped other gods, and his wife, Sarah, was barren, leaving them childless and without any hope of offspring. Even so, God chose Abraham to be not only a father of God's people but of the promised offspring, Jesus Christ. God appeared to Abraham and called him to leave his home and his family and follow the Lord. In His grace, God made three promises to Abraham. First, God promised to make Abraham's name great and his offspring innumerable. This man who was childless would have more children than he could count, numbering the stars in the sky or grains of sand on the seashore. He would become the father of a multitude of nations. God also promised land for his children to dwell in—a land of abundance and peace. Finally, God promised Abraham that through his offspring, all the nations of the world would be blessed. God's promise to Abraham did not stop with him but extended to every generation and nation of the world.

God made a covenant with Abraham—a binding and unbreakable agreement. Even when it seemed impossible, God's promises to Abraham were as steadfast and sure as the God who made them. God sealed the covenant with a ceremony showing that the fulfillment of the promises was entirely dependent on God. When nations formed covenants with one another, it was customary for the lesser nation to take an oath that it would receive a curse if it did not keep the terms of the covenant. In this ceremony, animals would be cut in two, and the pieces would be separated to form a pathway in the middle. The lesser nation would walk between the divided animals, symbolically saying, "So may God do to me and more also if I fail to keep the terms of this covenant." In God's covenant ceremony, it is not Abraham who passes through the pieces but God Himself. The curse of the covenant would not fall on Abraham, but God would take it upon Himself. Many generations later, the Son of God would become a baby born in a stable, the fullness of God in human form taking the curse on Himself. The sins of Abraham and all who put their faith in Jesus would be laid on Him, and He would become a curse and pay the penalty of death on the cross.

Jesus fulfills the curse of God's covenant with Abraham, but He also fulfills its promises. Through Jesus Christ, Abraham's offspring are not just those who share his DNA; all who have faith in Jesus are sons of Abraham and heirs of the promise. The land promised to Abraham would not just be the land of Canaan but the new heaven and new earth that Jesus will usher in at His second coming when all God's people will dwell with Him. Jesus Christ is the offspring of Abraham through whom all the nations of the world would be blessed. It is His life, death, and resurrection that enables people from every tribe, tongue, and nation to receive forgiveness and inherit eternal life with Him.

Abraham received the promise of God, but he would not see it fulfilled in his lifetime. Even so, Abraham believed the Lord. Even when it seemed impossible, God would fulfill every promise He made to Abraham in His way and timing, and He would do it through Jesus Christ. God told Abraham that kings would come from his offspring, and on that holy night in Bethlehem, the King of creation was born — Jesus the son of Abraham, Jesus the Son of God. As we look back to celebrate His birth, we also look forward with confidence that He will come again. God will bring about His promises in His way and timing, and He will do it through Jesus Christ.

ALL WHO HAVE FAITH IN JESUS
ARE SONS OF ABRAHAM AND
HEIRS OF THE PROMISE.

WHAT DOES THE FACT THAT GOD CHOSE ABRAHAM TO BE THE RECIPIENT OF SUCH A GREAT
PROMISE REVEAL ABOUT THE WAY GOD WORKS? HOW DOES THAT ENCOURAGE YOU TODAY?

WHAT DOES GOD'S COVENANT CEREMONY TEACH YOU ABOUT THE GOSPEL?

HAS THERE EVER BEEN A TIME WHEN YOU HAVE STRUGGLED TO TRUST IN GOD'S PROMISES
OR HIS TIMING? WRITE A PRAYER ASKING GOD TO STRENGTHEN YOUR FAITH.

01 / 04

Every detail of God's plan of redemption concerns Jesus Christ.

Isaac

Every detail of God's plan of redemption concerns Jesus Christ. Every part of Scripture points to Him. The story of Scripture is a story that builds toward the birth, life, death, resurrection, and sure second coming of Jesus. It is a divine story that progressively unfolds using real people in history. Abraham was a real person, and his family line was chosen by God to bring about Jesus, the Redeemer. From the very beginning, it is clear that God's plan is to glorify Himself through the use of humanly impossible circumstances.

When Abraham (then called Abram) received this unbreakable promise from God, he and his wife were without a biological heir. Abram's wife, Sarai, was barren. Yet, despite this glaring barrier to the fulfillment of God's promise of countless offspring that would include the Messiah, Abram believed. Against all logic, he trusted God, and for 24 years he lived and "called upon the name of the Lord" (Genesis 12:8). Those years required walking in faith as Sarai remained barren. There were moments of doubt. About a decade into the journey, Sarai gave her maidservant, Hagar, to Abram to bear a child named Ishmael. But God did not alter His plan. When Abram was 99 years old, God reaffirmed His promise to Abram and changed his name to Abraham, which means "father of many nations." He changed Sarai's name to Sarah, and He told them that they would conceive and have a son the following year. Abraham would be 100 years old, and Sarah would be 99 years old—she would be well past her childbearing years. Despite Abraham and Sarah's attempts to provide God an alternative solution to carrying out His promises, God reaffirmed the conditions by saying to Abraham, "No. Your wife Sarah will bear you a son, and you will name him Isaac. I will confirm my covenant with him as a permanent covenant for his future offspring" (Genesis 17:19). The promised child's conception would be miraculous. His very existence would be a reminder of the covenant-making and covenant-keeping God. Isaac was a glimpse of the Promised One, Jesus, whose conception would be miraculous and in whom every promise would be fulfilled. It would all happen just as God said.

At the appointed time, Sarah conceived and birthed Isaac. Despite decades of waiting, God was right on time. Despite the effects of the curse of sin on human bodies, God displayed His ability to bring life and fulfill His promises. Isaac was born, and it was undoubtedly clear that he was the one who would receive the Abrahamic covenant. Yet, God was not done. Years later, God called Abraham to sacrifice his only son, Isaac (Genesis 22:2, 12). Abraham, trusting in God's power to fulfill His word, immediately obeyed. Isaac trusted his father as he followed him to the altar without an animal sacrifice in tow. When it was time, Isaac did not fight against being tied to the wood as the sacrifice. And as Abraham raised his knife to kill his son, God was right on time and stopped him. God provided a substitutionary atonement—a ram.

Again, we are pointed to Jesus. Like Isaac, Jesus was a beloved, only son who willingly submitted to His Father's will. Like Isaac, Jesus did not fight against the wooden cross that He was called to bear. However, unlike Isaac, Jesus was the ram. He was sacrificed as the substitute offering, providing substitutionary atonement for all of God's people. Though He was without sin, He bore the wrath of His Father that our sins justly deserved. In doing so, He made a way for us to be recipients of every spiritual blessing. In the end, Jesus is the true and better Isaac.

Isaac played a key role in God's story as he was a part of Jesus's royal lineage. The Abrahamic covenant was carried on through Isaac and his offspring. It is this covenant that ultimately culminates in the Savior of the world. Jesus is the fulfillment of this everlasting covenant; He is the means by which the spiritual blessings of this covenant are given to the nations. The gospel did not start in the New Testament. It was proclaimed ahead of time to Abraham and then to Isaac and his offspring (Galatians 3:8). God's plan of redemption was not haphazardly executed. God's sovereign hand has always been involved, tending to details that go beyond human ability. On every branch of the family tree, we see this attribute of God hanging on display—that He is faithful, and He always follows through with His promises.

GOD'S SOVEREIGN HAND HAS ALWAYS BEEN INVOLVED, TENDING TO DETAILS THAT GO BEYOND HUMAN ABILITY.

THE CONCEPTION OF ISAAC WAS A MIRACLE BY ANY MEASURE. WHAT DO YOU LEARN ABOUT GOD'S CHARACTER FROM THIS ACCOUNT? HOW DOES IT STIR YOUR AFFECTIONS FOR CHRIST?

THROUGHOUT HISTORY, WE SEE A BEAUTIFUL DYNAMIC BETWEEN THE SOVEREIGNTY OF GOD AND THE LIVES OF REAL PEOPLE. HOW DO YOU SEE THIS DYNAMIC PLAYED OUT IN THE ACCOUNT OF ISAAC? HOW DO YOU SEE THIS PLAYED OUT IN YOUR OWN LIFE?

TAKE SOME TIME TO PRAY AND THANK GOD FOR BEING A PROMISE KEEPER. MAY THIS TIME OF REFLECTION AND RESPONSE STIR YOUR AFFECTIONS FOR CHRIST.

01 / 05

God has always delighted in using flawed, imperfect people for His glorious, good purposes.

Jacob

Jesus's family tree is full of interesting people. Though some are lauded for great faith, they all struggled with sin as we do. When we look at the individual stories of the people of Matthew 1, we might wonder why God chose to use such flawed and sinful men and women in His plan to send perfect, sinless Jesus. But God has always used sinful people to bring about His good purposes, teaching those He calls to Himself to know and fear Him, completely changing their lives in the process. Jacob is one of those people.

Born to Isaac and Rebekah after years of barrenness, Jacob was the answer to his father's prayer for a child. Jacob came into the world grasping the heel of his twin brother, Esau. His name, Jacob, means "he deceives," a trait that would follow him throughout his life, both as the deceiver and the deceived. Favored by his mother, Jacob was a quiet man who preferred the indoors. His twin was an outdoorsman favored by his father, Isaac. At the advice of his mother, Jacob impersonated his brother and tricked his father into endowing him with the blessing rightfully belonging to his firstborn twin. He had already manipulated Esau out of his birthright (a double inheritance earmarked for the firstborn son), and his deception only intensified the turmoil between the twins. After stealing Esau's blessing, Jacob fled from his family to avoid a confrontation.

What did God do with such a manipulative deceiver? He made Himself known to Jacob and promised to bless the world through his family. That response might not be what we expect, but God is unendingly kind and gracious to do good in the lives of people who do not deserve it. In His sovereignty, He chose to include Jacob in His promises to Abraham. If we learn anything from Jacob's story, we can see that God can use anything and anyone for His good purposes. While fleeing from his brother, Jacob stopped to rest at night on a pile of stones.

He dreamed of a ladder stretching from earth to heaven with angels descending up and down. The Lord stood above the ladder and addressed Jacob, making the same promise to him that He had made to Jacob's grandfather, Abraham. God told Jacob, "All the peoples on earth will be blessed through you and your offspring" (Genesis 28:14). God was reiterating the promise He had made to Abraham, showing Jacob that through his family, God would keep His covenant to bless the whole earth.

Unlike his father and grandfather, Jacob had a large family with twelve sons and one daughter. Though Abraham only had one son of promise, his offspring multiplied through Jacob's children. A family was becoming a nation. God changed Jacob's name to Israel, promising him, "a nation, indeed an assembly of nations, will come from you, and kings will descend from you" (Genesis 35:11). Jacob was changed—transformed by the presence and promises of God. He would no longer be known as the deceiver but as Israel. It was through Jacob's children that the nation of Israel would come, and it was through Jacob's children that our Savior, the forever King, would come.

Jacob lived for 147 years and as was the custom then, blessed his sons before his death. He kept the most important blessing for his third-born son, Judah, through whom God's promises of blessing would continue to be fulfilled.

Jacob's story includes deception, family turmoil, and unique experiences with God. He lived both as a deceiver and as one deceived. He also saw God face-to-face and lived to tell about it. Still, Jacob struggled greatly with fear, deceit, and favoritism, even into his old age. Why was such a man included in the genealogy of Jesus?

God has always delighted in using flawed, imperfect people for His glorious, good purposes. He can mold sinful people who live for themselves into people who recognize their desperation for God's nearness. After marrying, having children, and amassing wealth, Jacob recognized his dependence on God of whom he said, "He has been with me everywhere I have gone" (Genesis 35:3b). More than Jacob needed a wife or children or wealth, he needed atonement for his sins. The good news for Jacob—and us—is that one of his descendants would live perfectly and die sacrificially to provide atonement for sin. God did not send His Son to die for perfect, sinless people. Rather, He sent Jesus to die for imperfect, sinful people who are desperately in need of Him. That includes every single one of us.

Thankfully, Jesus came for the Jacobs of the world. Our struggles with sin will not thwart God's plan. Rather, God's good plan made a way for us to be forgiven for our sins and to be reconciled to Him. When we read of Jesus's birth in Bethlehem, we might forget the hundreds of years of longing that came before the Son of God was laid in a manger. Advent is not a celebration of God's last-minute fix for our problem of sin. Rather, during Advent, we celebrate that it was always God's plan to send Jesus. He chose to do so through a long line of imperfect, sinful people who point us to a perfect, sinless Savior. And because He always keeps His promises, we can look forward to the return of our perfect, sinless Savior who will come back for us.

WHY DO YOU THINK GOD USES UNLIKELY PEOPLE IN HIS STORY OF REDEMPTION? HOW DOES THAT ENCOURAGE YOU REGARDING YOUR INVOLVEMENT IN THE KINGDOM OF GOD?

IN GENESIS 32:22-32, JACOB WRESTLED WITH A MAN ALL NIGHT BEFORE DEMANDING A BLESSING FROM THE MAN. READ VERSE 30. WHO WAS JACOB WRESTLING WITH?

READ GENESIS 49:8-12. HOW DOES JACOB'S BLESSING OVER HIS SON, JUDAH, POINT TO THE COMING OF JESUS?

Jesus would be the true Vine who would remain faithful to God and carry out the purpose of Israel.

Judah

We may be familiar with predictions that Jesus would come from the tribe of Judah and the Lion of Judah, but we may be less familiar with the story of how unlikely Judah, the unchosen one of Jacob, came to have his name in the genealogy of Jesus.

Judah was the third son of Jacob from Leah. When she bore him, she said, "This time I will praise the Lord," and "she named him Judah" (Genesis 29:35). With every son born, Leah hoped that it would cause Jacob to love her more. However, when she gave birth to Judah, her heart was turned to the Lord as she gave praise to Him instead. The very naming of her son suggests that he would be set apart. He was not Jacob's favored son, but he would be the one through whom blessing would come to the world.

Judah was not without flaws. In Genesis 37, Joseph's brothers, including Judah, would grow jealous of him to the point of seeking to do him harm. Instead of killing him, they threw him in a pit and then sat down to eat. As they were eating, there was a caravan of Ishmaelites coming from Gilead. It was then that Judah suggested that they sell him to this group. Judah did not seek to save Joseph's life, but rather, he was out to profit for himself.

In the very next chapter, the story focuses on Judah. It is a strange interjection in the story of Joseph, but it is one that shows Judah's continued moral decline involving his daughter-in-law. His downward spiral culminates in his statement at the end of the chapter, "She is more in the right than I" (Genesis 38:26). Judah was not someone to look up to. He failed his brother, and he fell most shamefully as he took his daughter-in-law as a prostitute.

But, as God is so prone to do, He used Judah's failure to refine him. Later in Genesis, as he promised his father, Judah stepped up to stand in the place of a keeper—as one responsible for his brother, Benjamin (Genesis 43). The one who was so willing to sell his brother, Joseph, was now sacrificially offering himself up on behalf of Benjamin. Even this act of service points us to one greater who would come from Judah and who would sacrificially offer Himself up for His own brother. Judah whispers to us of Christ.

That would not be the only shadow of Christ in Judah. In Genesis 49:8-12, Judah received the blessing from Jacob. The blessing was full of promises that he would be victorious over enemies, honored by others, and carry royalty in his lineage. These blessings would be partially fulfilled in the life of Judah. The tribe of Judah would remain a united tribe despite oppression. Judah would rise up among his brothers, and royalty would lace this genealogy without end.

The greater fulfillment of these blessings is found in Christ. The scepter would be passed from Judah to David and ultimately, to Christ. In this blessing of Judah, we not only see the prophecy of Jesus's coming but also His death and finally, His ruling in His kingdom for all of eternity. In Revelation 5, John begins to weep because there is no one worthy to open the scroll—to bring God's promises to completion. As John feels the weight of this, an elder says to him, "Do not weep. Look, the Lion from the tribe of Judah, the Root of David, has conquered so that he is able to open the scroll and its seven seals" (Revelation 5:5).

In the last two verses of Jacob's blessing to Judah, there is a donkey's colt, a choice vine, garments washed in wine, and his vesture in the blood grapes. As people on this side of the cross, these images rightfully point us to Jesus. He would be the one to ride into the city on the back of a donkey. He would be the choice vine. Israel was to be the vine of God, but they were unfaithful to Him and therefore, incurred the judgment of God. But Jesus would be the true Vine who would remain faithful to God and carry out the purpose of Israel. He would be the one whose robe is dipped in blood (Revelation 19:13)—the One whose blood covers the unfaithfulness and sins of His people to reconcile them back to God, enabling them to live a life worthy of their calling.

How unlikely for the One who was prophesied in the blessing of Judah, the One whose kingdom would never end, the One to whom shall be the obedience of all people—to come as a baby in a manger! Yet, this is how God saw fit to bring redemption to the world, and He chose the Redeemer to come through a lineage of broken people, including Judah.

Judah would be named for praise, but the One who would come from him would be the only One truly worthy of praise.

HE CHOSE THE REDEEMER TO COME THROUGH
A LINEAGE OF BROKEN PEOPLE.

WHY DO YOU THINK GOD CHOSE THE LINE OF JUDAH TO BE THE LINEAGE OF JESUS?

READ 2 SAMUEL 7:12-16. HOW IS THE BLESSING OF JUDAH CARRIED DOWN THROUGH THE LINE OF JUDAH TO DAVID?

SPEND TIME IN PRAYER, PRAISING GOD FOR HIS GIFT TO US IN HIS SON. ASK HIM TO FILL YOUR HEARTS WITH WONDER AT THE COMING OF HIS SON THIS ADVENT SEASON AND ANTICIPATION FOR HIS SECOND ADVENT.

weekly reflection

SUMMARIZE THE MAIN PRINCIPLES YOU LEARNED.

WHAT DID YOU OBSERVE FROM THIS WEEK'S TEXT ABOUT GOD AND HIS CHARACTER?

WHAT DOES THIS WEEK'S PASSAGE REVEAL ABOUT THE CONDITION OF MANKIND AND YOURSELF?

HOW DO THESE PASSAGES POINT TO THE GOSPEL?

HOW SHOULD YOU RESPOND TO THESE PASSAGES? WHAT SPECIFIC
ACTION STEPS CAN YOU TAKE THIS WEEK TO APPLY THESE PASSAGES?

WRITE A PRAYER IN RESPONSE TO YOUR STUDY OF GOD'S WORD.
ADORE GOD FOR WHO HE IS, CONFESS SINS THAT HE REVEALED IN
YOUR OWN LIFE, ASK HIM TO EMPOWER YOU TO WALK IN OBEDIENCE,
AND PRAY FOR ANYONE WHO COMES TO MIND AS YOU STUDY.

peace

peace

peace

peace

peace

peace

02 / 01
CANDLE LIGHTING DAY

peace

THE SECOND CANDLE REPRESENTS THE PEACE
OFFERED TO US THROUGH CHRIST.

PRAYER

Jesus, You are our lasting peace. You hold the entire world together so that we do not have to, and in You, we find the quiet contentment our souls crave. We were overwhelmed with anxieties and crushed by pressures from every side. We were guilty, bound for a life eternally separated from You. But in Your perfect life, death, and resurrection, You destroyed the power of sin and death and paved the way for us to have everlasting peace with God. Thank You, Lord. In the chaos and hustle of this Christmas season, would You bring unity where there may be conflict, order where there is chaos, and quietness where there is strife? Bring rest to our weary souls and relief as we sojourn a moment longer on this earth. Guard our hearts and minds with Your perfect peace, and remind us that You are returning again. Come, Lord Jesus, come!

Prince of Peace

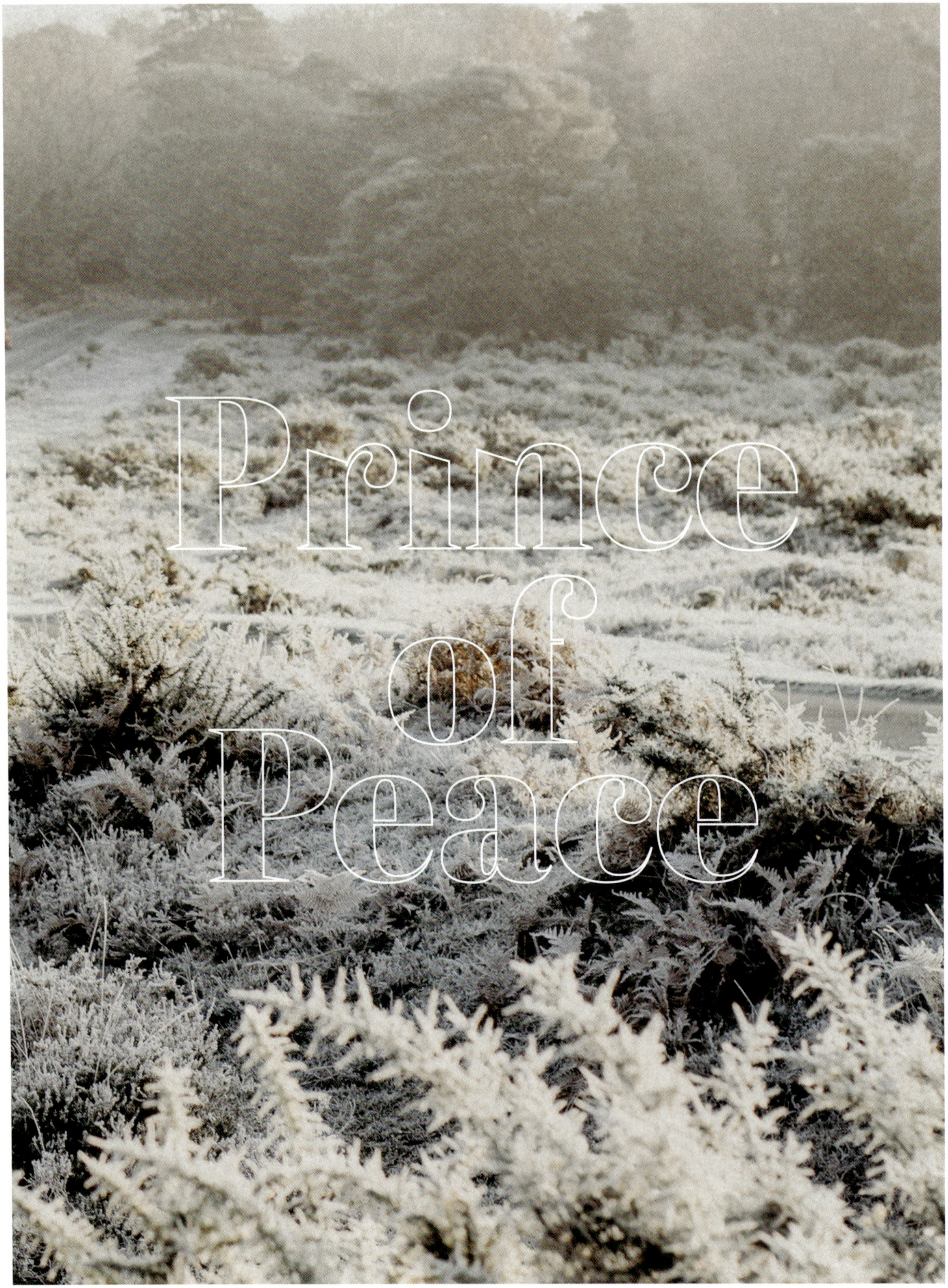

For a child will be born for us, a son will be given to us, and the government will be on his shoulders. He will be named Wonderful Counselor, Mighty God, Eternal Father, Prince of Peace.

ISAIAH 9:6

The family tree of
Christ is filled with every
kind of person and
every kind of story.

Tamar

Delving deeply enough into family history, along with the treasured and informative finds, we are also likely to uncover the messy and broken. The lineage of Jesus Christ exposes itself as a family like all the rest. As much as we may embrace certain elements of our family tree, there will undoubtedly be stories and memories to which we struggle to tie ourselves. Tamar's contribution is one of those stories that can be difficult and hard to remedy. But what we find at this place in the lineage is a story dripping with grace. The family tree of Christ is filled with every kind of person and every kind of story, which brings us to a great and glorious hope that by God's redemptive work through Christ, every kind of person with every kind of story is invited to come near.

Tamar is first introduced in Scripture as the wife to Er who was Judah and Shua's firstborn son and Jacob's grandson. However, Er was said to be "evil in the Lord's sight, and the Lord put him to death" (Genesis 38:7), making Tamar a widow. Adhering to the customs of a Levirate marriage, it was the duty of the deceased man's brother to marry his widow and bear offspring with her to preserve his brother's name and build up his brother's house (Deuteronomy 25:5-6). In this case, the responsibility fell on Er's brother, Onan, who did take Tamar as his wife. However, he refused to have a child with her because he was unwilling to give the child his deceased brother's name over his own. This displeased the Lord, so He also took Onan's life. After experiencing the death of two sons, Judah was overcome with grief and worried about what would happen should he give Tamar another of his sons to marry. So, he offered Tamar an empty promise of his son, Shelah, whenever he was old enough to be married. Tamar, now twice widowed, childless, and alone, agreed to this proposal and went to live in her father's house and remained a widow. Over time, it became evident that Judah had no intention of giving his son to marry Tamar, breaking his promise and neglecting his responsibility to Tamar as her father-in-law. He was avoiding the truth about his son's disobedience and the sin that ultimately led to their death and instead unfairly blamed Tamar. His denial and unwillingness to accept the shortcomings of his sons led to his own blatant disobedience.

This is when the story takes an uncomfortable turn. Judah's wife eventually passed away and left him grieving the loss of yet another loved one. Tamar heard of the news and remembered his unfulfilled promise to her. In retaliation, she found out where he was traveling, disguised herself as a prostitute, and waited for him to come by. When he finally passed by, Tamar offered to lie with him and covered her face so that he would not recognize her as his daughter-in-law. For temporary payment, she kept his signet ring, cord, and staff, which at that time served as something similar to an identification card, until he could provide her with proper payment. Little did Judah know, Tamar would become pregnant and provide his identification as a means of proving that he was the father. She had tricked him into performing the duties his sons should have but refused to. Though initially outraged and threatening to put Tamar to death, Judah was then overcome with guilt when she explained herself. He recognized not only the sins of his sons but the reality of his own failings in withholding Shelah from her, and he confessed it publicly to vindicate Tamar. She eventually gave birth to twins, Zerah and Perez, who would contribute to the continuation of the family line that brought forth Jesus Christ into the world.

Considering the difficulty of this story, we must take note of God's prevailing and unending mercy displayed. Even in the disobedience of Er and Onan, the injustice enacted by Judah, and the deception of Tamar, God's purposes were never thwarted. The consequences of their sin were not avoided, but God continued to work through these messiest, flawed, and sin-filled stories to accomplish His great and glorious purpose. God is the only one capable of providing a way out of the broken to that which will be made new. This is made possible through the fulfillment of God's promise to His people to send a perfect savior who would pave a way through the darkness of sin and bring us forth into glorious eternal life and light. This is the hope that enters through the birth of Jesus Christ—a hope offered to anyone who repents and believes in the Son of God as the Savior of the world. This is a hope that is offered to the one with a disrupted past, the one who bears the scars of trauma and tragedy, the one who has done the unthinkable, and the one who is the vilest of sinners.

The promise of Christ was brought forth through the most unthinkable circumstances to remind us that God would stop at nothing to fulfill it. He used Tamar's family to continue His faithful promise to His people, and He will continue to work redemptively through the lives of sinners to fulfill His good and perfect will, even now. This does not negate our need for repentance but leads us to it by directing our affections to God who bestows grace that is greater than our sin. May the recognition of this truth invite us to draw near to Christ this Advent season with all the baggage and burdens that follow us, leaning into His saving and sanctifying power and longing for His glorious return.

WHAT SURPRISES YOU ABOUT THE STORY OF TAMAR? HOW DOES HER STORY REVEAL THE HOPE
OF THE GOSPEL FOR SINNERS?

READ MATTHEW 1:3 AND LUKE 3:33. GOD CHOSE TAMAR, JUDAH, AND HER SONS, DESPITE THEIR
SIN, TO BE MENTIONED IN THE FAMILY LINE OF THE MESSIAH AND TO EACH HAVE THEIR ROLE IN
HIS PLAN OF REDEMPTION. WHAT DOES THIS TELL US ABOUT GOD'S CHARACTER?

HOW DOES THE STORY OF TAMAR AND HER FAMILY BRING TO LIGHT GOD'S UNFAILING
PLAN OF REDEMPTION? HOW DOES THIS BRING YOU COMFORT?

Without Christ,
we are all tarnished,
fallen, and desperate
for God's grace.

READ JOSHUA 2:1-21, 6:17-25, MATTHEW 1:5, HEBREWS 11:31, JAMES 2:25

Rahab

Of all the people listed in Jesus's family tree, we might be most surprised to find the name of a Gentile prostitute. How can the holy, sinless Son of God have such a tarnished, fallen woman in His ancestry? The story of Rahab should resonate with each of us because without Christ, we are all tarnished, fallen, and desperate for God's grace.

Rahab was a Canaanite woman who lived as a prostitute in the walled city of Jericho. Her home was not only a place men frequented for prostitution, but it was also a gathering place where news of the city circulated. God had promised to give the land of Canaan (where Jericho was located) to the people of Israel as their dwelling place. The only problem was that Jericho was a fortified city and nearly impossible to penetrate. Joshua, the leader of God's people at the time, sent two spies into Jericho to see what could be done about taking the city by force. The two spies lodged at the home of the town prostitute, Rahab. Why they stayed there, we do not know for certain. They could have sought out the wares she was offering, but it is more likely they could get news of the city at her home while blending in with the other men spending time there.

When the pagan king of Jericho heard that two Israelite spies were staying at Rahab's home, he sent word to have the men brought to him. Rahab, however, hid the men beneath some stalks of flax on her roof. She told the king she did not know the men were spies and had sent them on their way, urging the king's men to hurry after them. While the search party left the city to find the spies, Rahab kept them safely hidden away. Why would she turn on her king and hide the foreign spies? Rahab told the spies exactly why she hid them: "I know that the Lord has given you this land and that the terror of you has fallen on us, and everyone who lives in the land is panicking because of you" (Joshua 2:9). She went on to tell them that everyone in Jericho had heard how God had delivered Israel from slavery in Egypt and parted the Red Sea before them. They had also heard how God had defeated the mighty Amorites in the battle for Israel. When they heard all the deeds of Israel's God, they "lost heart, and everyone's courage failed...for the Lord your God is God in heaven above and on earth below" (Joshua 2:11).

Though Rahab had never had an encounter with Yahweh, Israel's God, she had heard about Him, and she believed that He was the only God. Rahab—an outsider, a Gentile, a woman, a prostitute—believed in God, and she was saved from destruction because of her faith. She promised the men to keep their espionage a secret if they would spare her and her family. Her home was built into the wall of the city, so using a red rope, she helped the spies escape out her exterior window. The spies promised to protect her and her family when they returned to take the city, telling her to drop the red rope out her window again so they would know which home was hers.

When the time came for Israel to take over Jericho, God gave them specific instructions to march around the city in silence once a day for six days. On the seventh day, they were to march around the city seven times, shouting and making noise during the last time around. After the final march, the strong city walls fell flat, opening up Jericho for destruction. Every person was killed except for Rahab and her family who were brought out of Jericho safely and kept outside the camp of Israel. Jericho was burned, and the land was taken by the people of God as He had promised them.

Rahab's entire family was saved as the spies had promised her, but that is not the end of Rahab's story. She was enfolded into the people of God, marrying a man named Salmon who was of the tribe of Judah. She is listed in the genealogy of Jesus as the mother of Boaz, which makes her the great-great-grandmother of King David. God included Rahab in His promise to bless the whole world through Abraham's family, for it was through Rahab's descendants that Jesus came.

Rahab is noted twice in the New Testament for her faith that motivated her to act in obedience to God whom she feared more than she feared man. We can learn from Rahab's life that anyone, regardless of ethnicity, background, or sinful past, can be included in God's family through faith. That is good news for us! There is nothing about our past or our background that is too much for God's grace to overcome. When we believe in Jesus for the atonement for our sins, we are enfolded into God's family by faith. And when we live by faith, our life will result in works of obedience to God. Real faith will be evidenced by real action, as it was in Rahab's life.

Rather than criticizing Rahab for her past, we should breathe a sigh of relief when we see her name in Jesus's genealogy. God has set His steadfast love on people from every tribe, nation, and language. We, too, are welcomed into His family simply by believing in His Son, Jesus Christ. Jesus's family includes people from all walks of life because He came for people from all walks of life. Like Rahab, God can save us from any sinful past. And like Rahab, we belong to Him when we live by faith in Him.

READ HEBREWS 11:31 AND JAMES 2:25. WHY DO YOU THINK RAHAB IS REFERRED TO AS "THE PROSTITUTE" IN THESE PASSAGES? WHAT CAN WE LEARN FROM HER LIFE?

HOW DID RAHAB PUT HER FAITH IN GOD INTO ACTION?

CONSIDERING THAT BOAZ'S MOTHER WAS A CANAANITE WOMAN FROM JERICHO, HOW DO YOU THINK THAT INFLUENCED THE WAY HE PERCEIVED RUTH, THE MOABITESS?

Not only was Ruth redeemed; she was grafted into the family tree of Jesus, the Messiah.

READ RUTH 1-4

Ruth

Women were not traditionally included in Hebrew genealogies, yet in the genealogy of Jesus, there are four women. Like Tamar and Rahab, the third woman in the genealogy, Ruth, was by all accounts an outcast. Though not sexually immoral, she was a Gentile, and she was from the nation of Moab, a persistent enemy of Israel. Her ethnicity would have naturally evoked unpleasant thoughts and feelings from the Israelites, yet God included such people in the royal heritage of the Messiah to attest to the nature of His grace extended to all sinners.

God empowered Moab to work against the Israelites because the "Israelites again did what was evil in the Lord's sight" (Judges 3:12). This oppression lasted for eighteen years, and it was during this time that the story of Ruth unfolded. Scripture tells us that an Israelite family moved to the land of Moab in response to a famine in the land of Judah. Ruth married one of the sons in this Israelite family, and for ten years, they lived in the land and remained childless. Then, all of the men in the family died. Naomi, the matriarch of the family, was suddenly left with two daughters-in-law, both without children and leaving them incredibly vulnerable and with no status in society. In light of the circumstances, Naomi urged these two women to return to their respective families. While one complied and left, Ruth refused. Naomi urged Ruth three times to go and find a better life for herself, but Ruth refused to leave her saying, "wherever you go, I will go, and wherever you live, I will live...May the Lord punish me, and do so severely, if anything but death separates you and me" (Ruth 1:16-17).

Though Ruth knew the disdain the Israelites would hold against her as a Moabitess, she returned to Bethlehem with Naomi. She was loyal to the family she married into and to the God of Israel who was now her God. Ruth was a widow and exile, but she was resolved. Despite her grief and uncertainties of her future, she was willing to work hard to provide for herself and her mother-in-law.

She began by picking grain from fields because it was the beginning of the harvest, and biblical law required field owners to leave behind whatever fell from the sheaves during the harvest for the poor to glean (Leviticus 23:22). It was by God's sovereignty that she picked from the fields of Boaz, a wealthy family relative of Naomi's late husband. Boaz was a generous and godly man who noticed Ruth and commended her faithfulness to her mother-in-law, even mentioning the personal cost at which it came. Boaz blessed Ruth and showed her favor by ensuring she picked ample grain, was protected from harm, and enjoyed proper provisions.

Naomi immediately recognized the aligning of these fortunate events as the lovingkindness and providence of God and told Ruth that Boaz was their family's kinsman-redeemer. Part of Israel's law stated that an unmarried man in an Israelite family should marry a widow within that family in order to provide for them—becoming a kinsman-redeemer, as in essence, he would redeem the family by marrying her and giving her a son to carry on the family name. Naomi encouraged Ruth to pursue Boaz, proposing a risky plan in which Ruth would essentially propose to Boaz during the night. Ruth obeyed her mother-in-law and said to Boaz, "Take me under your wing, for you are a family redeemer" (Ruth 3:9), mirroring Boaz's earlier prayer for her to receive her full reward from God, under whose wings Ruth had sought refuge (Ruth 2:12).

Boaz was a godly man who upheld the law and was willing to be the kinsman-redeemer, but he recognized that there was a closer relative who would rightfully fill this role. Thus, Boaz offered the opportunity to the closest relative, but when he heard about acquiring Ruth and carrying on her family name, he abandoned his right of redemption, allowing Boaz to purchase the property and marry Ruth. Scripture says, "the Lord granted conception to her, and she gave birth to a son" (Ruth 4:13). This child was Obed, the grandfather of King David. Not only was Ruth redeemed, but she was grafted into the family tree of Jesus, the Messiah.

There are many gospel elements in this story. Ruth was a Gentile from a nation that was an enemy of God and His people. Yet, God's grace has no bounds. It extends to all sinners; redemption is available to all who trust in the Lord. Boaz, as the kinsman-redeemer, was a type of Christ and had the ability and willingness to save Ruth and her family. Jesus is the only one with the ability to save us, and He willingly did so. At great cost to Himself, He made a way for the redemption of sinners. In Him, we are no longer enemies but children of God. No matter who we are, we can bring our emptiness and desperate need before the Lord and receive the fullness of His deliverance and provision. Whatever we may be facing, we can trust in the Lord's merciful providence and find shelter under His wings. He is always working to bring about His redemptive purposes.

GOD'S GRACE HAS NO BOUNDS.

READ JUDGES 2:16-19 TO GET A CLEARER CONTEXT OF THE STORY OF RUTH. DESPITE ISRAEL'S DISOBEDIENCE, GOD CONTINUED TO WORK IN BRINGING ABOUT HIS PLAN OF REDEMPTION. HOW DOES THIS ENRICH YOUR UNDERSTANDING OF GOD'S SOVEREIGNTY AND GOODNESS?

RUTH RESPONDED TO GOD'S GRACE BY PUTTING HER FAITH IN HIM, BUT SHE DID NOT STOP THERE. HOW DID RUTH ACT ON HER FAITH IN GOD? HOW DOES THIS ENCOURAGE YOU TO LIVE OUT YOUR FAITH?

SPEND SOME TIME IN PRAYER. BRING YOUR EMPTINESS, NEEDS, AND DESIRES BEFORE THE LORD, FINDING COMFORT UNDER HIS WINGS AND A REMINDER THAT HE IS STILL WORKING.

The seed that was promised, the true King, would appear and deliver God's people once and for all.

Jesse

A name that prominently stands out in the genealogy of Christ is Jesse. Some observe Advent with a Jesse Tree in which ornaments represent the family tree of Christ. This name is found in the well-known prophecy of Isaiah that the promised Messiah would be born into his family, the root of Jesse. This prophecy was welcomed by those who found themselves surrounded by kingdom destruction and demise, awaiting God's continued promise of restoration to His people. This prophecy provided a glimmer of hope in an otherwise hopeless world — that God would send a savior to deliver His people through the bloodline of Jesse: "Then a shoot will grow from the stump of Jesse, and a branch from his roots will bear fruit. The Spirit of the Lord will rest on him — a Spirit of wisdom and understanding, a Spirit of counsel and strength, a Spirit of knowledge and of the fear of the Lord" (Isaiah 11:1-2).

Jesse was the son of Obed and the grandson of Ruth and Boaz. He resided in Bethlehem as a farmer and sheep breeder with eight sons. One day, God sent the prophet Samuel to the house of Jesse, enlisted with the purpose of naming a chosen king from Jesse's sons. Upon arrival, Jesse was likely struck by the reason for Samuel's visit, honored to hear that one of his sons had been chosen by God for such a royal bestowment. He proudly presented his first seven sons one by one, but to his surprise, none were chosen. Finally, Samuel inquired about any remaining sons, and after learning of David, asked that he be retrieved. When Jesse presented his youngest son, David, Samuel named him as God's chosen one and anointed him in the presence of his brothers.

God instituted a line of kingly heirs through Jesse's son, David, from which He would bring forth the promised seed (Genesis 3:15, 2 Samuel 7:12) who would establish His throne and kingdom of peace forever. However, this establishment does not come without more devastation. Isaiah's prophecy lends purposeful terminology in that only a stump would remain of the root of Jesse. The people of God would continue to face hardship, and David's kingly line would decline to such a degree that they were essentially left for dead. Biblically recorded, David's royal dynasty would face near desolation as a result of God's judgment through Assyria and Babylon. Yet, Isaiah's prophecy told of life to spring forth—a shoot, that would emerge from his line into a mighty tree. The seed that was promised, the true King, would appear and deliver God's people once and for all.

The fulfillment of Isaiah's prophecy took place in the small town of Bethlehem hundreds of years later, where all who belonged to the house of David were required to go for a census to be taken. Mary and Joseph, belonging to his house, traveled from Nazareth to register. This was the providential means by which Jesus Christ, the promised Messiah, was born in the simple town of Bethlehem. Being born of the root of Jesse reminds us of the humanity of Jesus and His humble origins. As a shepherd from Bethlehem, Jesse occupied a relatively low and ordinary place in life. Yet through his everyday faithfulness, God used him to carry out His plan of redemption. When Christ was born, He would become the rightful heir to the throne of David, and as the prophecy foretold, "the root of Jesse will stand as a banner for the peoples. The nations will look to him for guidance, and his resting place will be glorious" (Isaiah 11:10).

On that day, hope was born. Jesus Christ is the shoot, or branch, born of the root of Jesse that redeemed the story of Israel and more-so offers redemption to us. Through His life, death, and resurrection, He provides a blood-bought invitation into His family. Those who receive the good news of the gospel, repenting and trusting in Jesus as their Savior, now find themselves grafted into the family of God, no longer as aliens or slaves but as brothers to Christ and children of God, which surpasses all other bloodlines. What a gift of grace—such a gift, that we should offer the message of this invitation freely and generously to all who will receive it. And one day, when Christ returns, all of God's family will gather together under the banner of His name, and the entire world will bow down before Him as He establishes His throne forever, just as the prophets foretold. Until then, we wait with great hope, knowing that no matter our surroundings or dry and desolate circumstances, the tree of Christ, established from the root of Jesse, ever remains firmly planted and bearing fruit. May we plant ourselves deeply in the heart of Christ this Advent season, clinging to the hope He brings and looking expectantly to the ways He will use us to further His kingdom to come.

THIS PROPHECY PROVIDED A GLIMMER OF HOPE IN AN OTHERWISE HOPELESS WORLD.

THOUGH JESSE'S STORY SEEMED ORDINARY, HOW DID GOD USE IT FOR EXTRAORDINARY PURPOSES? HOW MIGHT WE BE TEMPTED TO OVERLOOK GOD AT WORK IN THE ORDINARY ASPECTS OF OUR LIVES?

WHAT SIGNIFICANCE IS FOUND IN THE TERM "STUMP OF JESSE"?

THE MESSAGE OF THE GOSPEL SERVES AS AN INVITATION TO BE GRAFTED INTO GOD'S FAMILY. WHAT OPPORTUNITIES MIGHT PRESENT THEMSELVES TO SHARE THE GOSPEL THIS SEASON? WHO SPECIFICALLY CAN YOU BE PRAYING WOULD RECEIVE THE MESSAGE OF THE GOSPEL?

**The King is coming again,
and we look forward
to His return!**

David

As we continue through the lineage of Christ, we find King David's name. David, the smallest shepherd boy in his family and insignificant by most people's standards, was chosen by God to become the king of Israel as a man after God's own heart (1 Samuel 13:14). Young David was used by God to defeat the enemies of Israel, starting with the famous giant, Goliath, and continuing to Israel's neighboring enemies. He became so successful in battle that men wrote songs about him, and 2 Samuel 8:14 tells us, "The Lord made David victorious wherever he went." Loved and revered by many, David was also a gifted writer with a deep prayer life, writing most of the book of Psalms.

Yet, while David's life included extraordinary mountaintops, it also contained heartbreaking valleys. One day while his armies were in battle, David stayed home and saw a beautiful woman bathing on her roof. What started as a moment of lust led him down a path of adultery, conspiracy, attempted cover-ups, and murder. Later in his life, his absent parenting and lack of discipline led to abuse, division, and murder within his family. These failures culminated in an attempted coup by one of his sons. The power of sin and its enticing destruction was so pervasive that no one was immune, not even a man after God's own heart.

In the midst of his transgressions, David repented and experienced God's abundant forgiveness (Psalm 51). While his relationship with God was restored through confession and repentance, it was clear that this promising leader had fallen short. He was not the Promised One for whom Israel had been waiting. Unable to save himself, he looked forward to the One who was to come. Despite David's sin, God was determined to bring redemption to His people. In an act of incredible mercy, God chose David as his own and gave him an unbreakable covenant. He selected David to be grafted into the lineage of Christ, not because he was perfect but because God loved him. We see this covenant in

2 Samuel 7:8-17 when David's love for God propelled him to action; he wanted to do something great for the Lord. David regretted that he lived in a beautiful temple while the ark of the covenant, representing God's presence, was still in a tent. David determined to build God a house, but God flipped the tables and promised to build David a house instead. Through the prophet Nathan, God spoke to David, saying in 2 Samuel 7:11-13:

> *"The Lord declares to you: The Lord himself will make a house for you. When your time comes and you rest with your fathers, I will raise up after you your descendant, who will come from your body, and I will establish his kingdom. He is the one who will build a house for my name, and I will establish the throne of his kingdom forever."*

God promised not only to build David a house but also to establish his kingdom forever. This promise would be partially fulfilled through David's son, Solomon, who would build a temple for the Lord and continue the royal family line. More than this, though, it looked forward to the coming of the Messiah, when God would crush the head of the serpent (Genesis 3:15) and bring redemption to His people.

Indeed, the Promised One was coming who would break the power of sin, releasing its deadly grip on our hearts. This coming King would also come from humble beginnings, being born in a lowly manger to a poor virgin woman. Like David, He would face betrayal, hunger, and abuse. He would have no place to lay His head. Yet, He did it all without sin and for the glory of the Father.

Fully God and fully man, Jesus is the true and better David. He is the Good Shepherd who willingly left the splendor of heaven to seek and save His lost sheep. When faced with temptation, He endured faithfully to the end, never having a sinful, lustful, or impure motive. He was the spotless Lamb who took our sin upon Himself and paid for the wrath that we deserved. He went to the poor, the sick, and the needy to proclaim the good news of salvation for all who would repent and believe in Him. He was the perfect temple; He is God with us. He is our perfect, righteous King.

This King is coming again. And when He comes, He will lead His people with perfect justice and purity. As we long for Jesus's return, we should also evaluate our hearts. As we see in the life of David, God is gracious and merciful to forgive us of our sins when we come to Him. He promises that all who come to Him, repenting of their sins and believing in Him will find great mercy. This should be a great encouragement for us and spur us to action and worship. The King is coming again, and we look forward to His return!

HE SELECTED DAVID TO BE GRAFTED INTO THE LINEAGE OF CHRIST, NOT BECAUSE HE WAS PERFECT BUT BECAUSE GOD LOVED HIM.

HOW DOES DAVID'S LIFE ILLUSTRATE THE NEED FOR A PERFECT SAVIOR?

READ PSALM 51. WHEN DAVID SINNED, HE REPENTED AND FOUND FORGIVENESS IN THE LORD. IF YOU HAVE ANY UNCONFESSED SIN, SPEND TIME REPENTING AND ASKING FOR THE LORD'S FORGIVENESS.

HOW DOES THE DAVIDIC COVENANT PROPHESY THE COMING OF CHRIST (2 SAMUEL 7:8-17)?

weekly reflection

SUMMARIZE THE MAIN PRINCIPLES YOU LEARNED.

WHAT DID YOU OBSERVE FROM THIS WEEK'S TEXT ABOUT GOD AND HIS CHARACTER?

WHAT DOES THIS WEEK'S PASSAGE REVEAL ABOUT THE CONDITION OF MANKIND AND YOURSELF?

HOW DO THESE PASSAGES POINT TO THE GOSPEL?

HOW SHOULD YOU RESPOND TO THESE PASSAGES? WHAT SPECIFIC
ACTION STEPS CAN YOU TAKE THIS WEEK TO APPLY THESE PASSAGES?

WRITE A PRAYER IN RESPONSE TO YOUR STUDY OF GOD'S WORD.
ADORE GOD FOR WHO HE IS, CONFESS SINS THAT HE REVEALED IN
YOUR OWN LIFE, ASK HIM TO EMPOWER YOU TO WALK IN OBEDIENCE,
AND PRAY FOR ANYONE WHO COMES TO MIND AS YOU STUDY.

JOY
JOY
JOY
JOY
JOY
JOY
JOY

03 / 01
CANDLE LIGHTING DAY

joy

THE THIRD CANDLE OF ADVENT REPRESENTS
THE JOY WE FIND IN CHRIST.

PRAYER

Jesus, You are our greatest joy. We thank You because You came down to earth and lived among us. As a baby You cried, ate, slept, and grew, joining us in the everyday experience of human existence. You matured into adulthood and became a man who led others with perfect wisdom, strength, and grace. When the perfect time had come, and for the joy set before You, Jesus, You endured the cross, scorning its shame, and sat down at the right hand of the Father. You have saved us and secured our eternal future through Your finished work on the cross. You have set us free, bringing us from darkness to light, and You have put more joy in our hearts than any earthly thing. Though we cannot see You, we love You and rejoice with inexpressible joy knowing that one day, we will see You again. This joy is not dependent on our changing circumstances or the number of presents under the Christmas tree. It is secured through Jesus. Though the sorrows may last in this long, dark night, Your joy will surely come again in the morning. Thank You for Your sacrificial love, Lord. You are all we need.

great
joy

*But the angel said to them,
"Don't be afraid, for look,
I proclaim to you good news
of great joy that will be for
all the people: Today in the
city of David a Savior was
born for you, who is the
Messiah, the Lord.*

LUKE 2:10-11

03 / 02

Yet again, we have
an opportunity for God
to remind us of how
faithful He remains to
His promises.

Uriah, Bathsheba, and Solomon

In the genealogy of Jesus, not all names are listed in the same way. For instance, some simply use the word "fathered" (ex. Abraham fathered Isaac) while still others include several important variations like naming the mother as well. And within these names, we find a jarring description: "David fathered Solomon by Uriah's wife." Scripture helps us to identify Uriah's wife in the Old Testament as a woman named Bathsheba, but the purposeful wording of the recorded genealogy highlights another scandal in the lineage of Jesus. Yet again, we have an opportunity for God to remind us of how faithful He remains to His promises.

Uriah, a Hittite, was one of King David's most trusted military officers, even referred to as one of his "Mighty Men." He was married to Bathsheba who was described as a very beautiful woman. One spring, David sent out his troops and officers to war but decided he would stay back in Jerusalem. While they were away, David took an evening stroll on his roof and caught a glimpse of a woman bathing. Seemingly taking advantage of his royal status, he sent messengers to retrieve her to sleep with him, even after learning of her identity as another man's wife, Bathsheba. Following the adulterous act, likely ridden with guilt and shame, David sent Bathsheba back home. She soon learned she was pregnant with David's child and sent news to warn him. To cover up the affair, David sent for Uriah to temporarily return to Jerusalem in hopes that he would sleep with Bathsheba and think the conceived child was his own. However, Uriah was a loyal and dedicated soldier. He refused to sleep with his wife while his fellow soldiers were still fighting on the battlefield, and he instead slept at the front door of the palace with servants. David then devised a new plan to order that Uriah return to war and be placed on the front lines of battle so that he would be killed. News returned of Uriah's death, and David responded with seeming complacency, while Bathsheba mourned the loss of her husband.

Eventually, David married Bathsheba, and she bore him a son. But the Lord considered David's actions evil in His sight. The consequences of David's sin would continue to follow him and his family. And yet, God's mercy would abound as He sent the prophet Nathan to confront David in his sin. Nathan went to David and presented a parable of a selfish, rich man stealing from a poor man. Hearing this, David was provoked to anger, saying to Nathan, "the man who did this deserves to die!" In which Nathan responded, "You are the man!" David immediately recognized and was convicted of his sin, leading him to confess and repent to the Lord. God, in His great mercy, had orchestrated how David would be led to repentance. And it was only by God's grace that David saw evidence of his dark and disobedient ways. Though David's sin would continue to bear heartbreaking and devastating consequences, including the death of Bathsheba's son, God would bring redemption and restoration. He would even bless David and Bathsheba with another son, Solomon, who would one day take the throne of David as his chosen heir.

When Solomon was born, Scripture tells us that "The Lord loved him" (2 Samuel 12:24). There was something significant about this child. He would not be the only son of David, but he would be the chosen one to inherit the throne and be the next king of Israel. Though there would be competition for the throne, David appointed Solomon to become king (1 Kings 1:35). In agreement, Benaiah son of Jehoiada said, "May the Lord, the God of my lord the king, so affirm it. Just as the Lord was with my lord the king, so may he be with Solomon and make his throne greater than the throne of my lord King David" (1 Kings 1:36-37).

Solomon followed in the footsteps of his father and knew that the blessing of his leadership depended on the Lord. David had given him instructions on his deathbed saying,

> *"Be strong and be a man, and keep your obligation to the Lord your God to walk in his ways and to keep his statutes, commands, ordinances, and decrees...so that the Lord will fulfill his promise that he made to me: 'If your sons take care to walk faithfully before me with all their heart and all their soul, you will never fail to have a man on the throne of Israel'" (1 Kings 2:2-4).*

This is the promise God made to David, and this promise was carried on through the kingship of Solomon.

In the early years of his kingship over Israel, the Lord appeared to Solomon and asked Solomon, "What should I give to you?" (1 Kings 3:5). After Solomon acknowledged all that God had given him, he asked for "a receptive heart to judge your people and to discern between good and evil" (1 Kings 3:9). Solomon did not request riches or fame or life or death of his enemies. Instead, he asked for wisdom. And God granted him "a wise and understanding heart" so that there had been none like him before and never would be again (1 Kings 3:12).

God not only granted him wisdom, but he lavishly gave him everything he had not sought. Solomon was unlike any other ruler in his day. The renown of his wisdom went forth among all nations, and so much so that "Emissaries of all peoples, sent by every king on earth who had heard of his wisdom, came to listen to Solomon's wisdom" (1 Kings 4:34). He was a great man. He would be the one who partially fulfilled the promise made to David. He built a house for the Lord and reigned on the throne.

Though his wisdom surpassed anyone in his day, there was one greater still to come. In Matthew

12:42 Jesus said, "The queen of the south will rise up at the judgment with this generation and condemn it, because she came from the ends of the earth to hear the wisdom of Solomon; and look—something greater than Solomon is here." That something—someone—was Jesus. Jesus is greater than Solomon. Jesus not only has wisdom; He is wisdom. Jesus "became wisdom from God for us—our righteousness, sanctification, and redemption" (1 Corinthians 1:30). And "In him are hidden all the treasures of wisdom and knowledge" (Colossians 2:3). If we would be wise and seek knowledge, it is not degrees and diplomas we need; we need mainly to press into Christ, who is greater than Solomon and the sum of all wisdom.

HOW DOES THE STORY OF DAVID AND BATHSHEBA LEAD YOU TO UNDERSTAND THE ABOUNDING GRACE OF GOD? HOW DOES IT ENCOURAGE YOU TO RECEIVE GOD S GRACE TODAY?

WALK THROUGH I KINGS 1-3, AND HIGHLIGHT THE JOURNEY OF SOLOMON IN BECOMING A KING. WHERE DO YOU SEE THE LORD'S HAND IN THIS?

WHAT DOES COLOSSIANS 2:3 MEAN? HOW IS JESUS WISDOM INCARNATE?.

Jesus overcomes our foolishness and limited wisdom. He redeems all of our failures.

The Line of Kings

The southern kingdom of Judah is the line that we find in the genealogy of Christ in Matthew 1. The lineage begins with Rehoboam: "Rehoboam fathered Abijah, Abijah fathered Asa, Asa fathered Jehoshaphat, Jehoshaphat fathered Joram, Joram fathered Uzziah, Uzziah fathered Jotham, Jotham fathered Ahaz, Ahaz fathered Hezekiah, Hezekiah fathered Manasseh, Manasseh fathered Amon, Amon fathered Josiah" (Matthew 1:7b-10). This genealogy was not exhaustive; many names were omitted. In fact, three kings are missing between Joram and Uzziah (Azariah), all of whom were evil and died violently. But the list given serves a distinct purpose for Matthew and his hearers. The Jewish people had awaited a Messiah, and they knew this Messiah was to come from the line of David. Therefore, Matthew traces Jesus's genealogy through a series of kings who stem from David, proving that Jesus is the Messiah. He is the Promised One of David's lineage.

There is a long line of kings, and our focus for today includes the kings found between Solomon and Josiah's reign. In this series of kings, some did right in the eyes of the Lord, but unfortunately, the bad kings far outweighed the good. Some of the names woven into Jesus's lineage did have their eyes set on the Lord, but even then, they were not perfect. They would still bear the mark of sin as every human has since the fall of Adam and Eve. But even though some were good, we cannot overlook how evil the other kings were who we find in this genealogy of Jesus.

Solomon took the throne after his father, David, and he reigned as king over the united kingdom of Israel until his death. At his death, his son, Rehoboam, took the throne (1 Kings 12:1-24). But this would be the last king who ruled over the kingdom of Israel as one, and he would do so in the way of David and Solomon for three years (2 Chronicles 11:17). The kingdom of God's people was entrusted to him. God's people were in the Promised Land under God's rule under the leadership of the king. This was the closest God's people had been to a kingdom under God's rule since Genesis 2 when Adam and Eve were in fellowship with God, in His place, and under His rule and blessing. But Rehoboam would prove to be a wicked king. After only three years under the kingship of Rehoboam, the kingdom was divided into two: the northern kingdom of Israel and the southern kingdom of Judah. Rehoboam lost the kingdom that was entrusted to him, and he lost it because of his foolishness. Instead of listening to the wise counsel that surrounded his father, he chose to listen to young men. The mark of his folly would remain on the people of Israel. None of the kings of Israel were good; they neglected to worship and follow God. Out of the twenty kings of the southern kingdom of Judah, only a few would be good.

And so the line continues. Manasseh, though his father did good in the sight of the Lord, may be the worst king of them all. Manasseh did what was evil in the sight of the Lord. He reestablished idol worship, rebuilt altars to false gods, "sacrificed his son in the fire, practiced witchcraft and divination, and consulted mediums and spiritists" (2 Kings 21:6). The writer of Kings concludes, "He did a huge amount of evil in the Lord's sight" (2 Kings 21:6). And his son, Amon, would follow in his wicked ways. Though directly about Amon, perhaps 2 Kings 21:21-22 gives the best summary statement for the succession of kings that we have: "He walked in all the ways his father had walked; he served the idols his father

had served, and he bowed in worship to them. He abandoned the Lord God of his ancestors and did not walk in the ways of the Lord."

The names of Rehoboam, Abijah, Joram, Ahaz, Manasseh, and Amon should give us great hope and encouragement. God could have chosen His Son to be born through a righteous line, but He did not. Instead, He used sinful, wicked people in the lineage of Jesus. And to think that God would choose this kind of people to carry out His plan to redeem the world! What great mercy and compassion the Lord has on mankind.

Israel wanted a king, and God gave them what they asked for. But the kings who would sit on the throne of Israel would leave the people unsatisfied. They would not accomplish what the people had hoped. Some would rule wickedly. Some would treat others unjustly. Some would even use their power to harm those under their care. All of this would cause the people to long for one to come who would be better—a king who would come and rule justly, with equity and righteousness. God would send Jesus to be the true King. Where Rehoboam reigned in foolishness, and his folly would remain in infamy, Jesus comes and reigns with wisdom. Rehoboam may have lost the kingdom, but Jesus is the wise King who came to restore it all. Through Jesus's wisdom, the kingdom of God is at hand. Jesus overcomes our foolishness and limited wisdom. He redeems all of our failures. He inaugurated the kingdom, and He will one day restore the kingdom of God completely in the new heaven and new earth.

GOD WOULD SEND JESUS TO
BE THE TRUE KING.

WHY DO YOU THINK GOD USES BAD, WICKED KINGS IN THE LINEAGE OF JESUS?

HOW DOES THE WORLD AROUND YOU CAUSE YOU TO LONG FOR KING JESUS?

READ PSALM 99. WRITE OUT A PRAYER, PRAISING GOD THAT HE IS KING.

Josiah's name, which means, "healed of the Lord" or "the Lord will support," pointed to the healing and restoration God would bring to the land during Josiah's lifetime.

Josiah

Josiah was only eight years old when he became king of Judah. For over seventy years before him, Josiah's dad and grandfather had wickedly ruled over the land. His grandfather, Manassah, was an especially evil king, credited for turning the people away from God and promoting idolatrous worship. But even as a youth, Josiah did not follow the ways of his fathers; instead, he wanted to please God. He started seeking the Lord at sixteen years old, and by twenty, he rid the land of its idols and Asherah poles. Josiah's name, which means, "healed of the Lord" or "the Lord will support," pointed to the healing and restoration God would bring to the land during Josiah's lifetime.

As he grew, Josiah continued to obey the Lord, and when he was 26 years old, he decided to restore the temple of God which had since come to ruins. While men were cleaning up the temple, they found the Word of God which had been lost. Incredulously, God's Word, which had faithfully guided the people for years had been thoughtlessly discarded and ignored by the kings before him. As Josiah read it, he became convicted of the sins of the people and tore his clothes, a sign of grieving at the time. Josiah knew that the people had disobeyed God's commands and that consequences were coming because of their rebellion. He sought the counsel of a prophetess who spoke God's coming judgment over the people. But because of Josiah's desire to please the Lord, God showed mercy to him and promised peace during Josiah's reign. Josiah continued to follow God's commands and led the people in obeying the Passover, and for the rest of Josiah's days, the people followed the Lord.

While a godly man, Josiah was not perfect. At the end of his life, he too disregarded God's wisdom and lost his life as a result. Through the pharaoh, Neco, God told Josiah not to go to battle, but Josiah disobeyed and, under disguise, went to battle anyway. He was shot by an arrow and died. Even the best leaders of history fail. Every one of Israel's kings was sinful, and from Josiah's story, we can observe how significantly leaders influence their people. When the kings obeyed the Lord, the people followed. When the kings rebelled, the people were quick to pick up their Asherah poles and worship idols instead of the Lord. Josiah's life points to the need for a perfect ruler—one who would lead his people in grace and truth.

Indeed, the perfect King was coming. Hundreds of years later, in a small, dirty stable, Jesus would come as a perfect little baby. Though born into circumstances seemingly unfit for a king, Jesus too was born into the royal lineage, King at His birth. But unlike Josiah, Jesus would obey God's law faultlessly, even unto death. He desired to do the will of the Father, and unlike all the kings before him, would lead His people in complete humility, wisdom, and justice.

Jesus is the true and better King who not only would grieve over the sins of His people but also have the power to change hearts. Jesus not only obeyed the Father perfectly, but He also led His people to repentance and obedience, making a way for us to be saved. Whereas Josiah would lead the people to celebrate the Passover, Jesus Himself became the Passover Lamb. He bore the sins of His people on the cross and paid the substitutionary sacrifice that we deserved. While Josiah's reign brought with it temporary healing and restoration, we now can live forever restored to God through the perfect life, death, and resurrection of Christ.

Just as Josiah chose a path that was different from that of his father and his grandfather, we too must decide whether to submit to Jesus's lordship over our lives, regardless of the decisions of those around us. Each person is responsible before the Lord for his or her own decisions. We are never too young or too old to repent and experience the mercy of God.

This Christmas, let us worship the perfect King, the Passover Lamb who flawlessly obeyed God's commands. Just as the Israelites were quick to wander, so are we. Let us follow His leadership and submit ourselves to a Bible-believing, local church that can instruct us and lead us in accordance with the truths found in God's Word. Jesus has come as the fulfillment of the promise to purchase and redeem His bride. And He is coming again! He will reveal all the secret disguises of our hearts and lead His children under His humble and righteous rule. Worthy is our King, the spotless Passover Lamb.

THOUGH BORN INTO CIRCUMSTANCES SEEMINGLY UNFIT FOR A KING, JESUS TOO WAS BORN INTO THE ROYAL LINEAGE, KING AT HIS BIRTH.

HOW DOES THE LIFE OF JOSIAH POINT TO THE NEED FOR A PERFECT KING?

FROM THE STORIES OF THE ISRAELITE KINGS, WE SEE THAT OUR LEADERS GREATLY INFLUENCE US. WHO IS LEADING YOU, AND ARE YOU BEING LEAD TO OR AWAY FROM GOD'S WORD

GOD'S WORD WAS LOST FOR MANY YEARS, AND UPON READING IT, JOSIAH WAS CONVICTED AND WEPT. HOW DOES GOD'S WORD CONVICT AND GUIDE YOU IN YOUR DAILY LIFE?

CHRIST IS OUR PASSOVER LAMB. HAVE YOU SUBMITTED TO HIS LORDSHIP, REPENTING OF YOUR SINS AND TRUSTING IN HIS SUFFICIENT SACRIFICE? WHY OR WHY NOT?

God was still patient
with the Judahites.
He allowed generations
of time to turn
back to Him.

Exile and Deportation to Babylon

The wicked reign of four successive kings followed King Josiah. Unlike Josiah, these men did not exhibit godly leadership or zeal for the Lord. Instead, the kings continued the sinful ways of their ancestor, Manasseh. As cited in 2 Kings 21, Judah's King Manasseh built altars for pagan gods, consulted witches, and even sacrificed his own son in exchange for more power. Manasseh also established idol statues in the temple and led the people astray with his idolatry. The people of Judah disregarded the Lord's standard for holiness and proved to have unfaithful hearts. Because of the corruption in Judah under King Manasseh, the Lord declared He would give the Israelites over to their enemies and to the spiritual darkness they desired. And, the Lord would exercise His good and righteous judgment in the fall of Judah.

But, God was still patient with the Judahites. He allowed generations of time to turn back to Him. But, unfortunately, King Jehoahaz, Jehoiakim, Jehoiachin, and Zedekiah, remained hard-hearted, and their power slowly succumbed to stronger nations. The Lord's patience came to an end. Nebuchadnezzar and his Babylonian army besieged Jerusalem. They ransacked and plundered the temple. Thousands were captured, leaving only the poorest in Judah. God's people were exiles, dragged away from the land the Lord had graciously gifted them. With no king to protect her, Jerusalem, the once beautiful city-temple of God, was destroyed and burned to the ground.

The kings of Judah did not listen to the prophet Jeremiah who spoke the Lord's words and declared, "I will gather them and bring them to an end...There will be no grapes on the vine, no figs on the fig tree, and even the leaf will wither. Whatever I have given them will be lost to them" (Jeremiah 8:13). Like Jeremiah prophesied, the Promised Land was desolate. This state reflected the loss of covenant blessings and the lifelessness of sin. As a result, the Israelites mourned in Babylon and prayed for the Lord to restore them. Sounds of lament filled the air as the Israelites longed for the King of kings—God Himself—to rescue them from their sinful nature. In their grief, through Jeremiah, the Lord spoke a message of hope and healing. The Lord declared, "I will restore the fortunes of Judah and of Israel and will rebuild them as in former times. I will purify them from all the iniquity they have committed against me, and I will forgive all the iniquities they have committed against me, rebelling against me" (Jeremiah 33:7-8). God promised to draw those exiled in sin back to Himself and assured He would preserve a faithful remnant and bring peace through His kingdom to come.

The Lord affirmed His covenant with King David (Jeremiah 33:14-17). He would raise a King from David's line, and His throne would be eternal. Unlike the sinful kings of Judah and Israel, this king would be truly good, and His righteousness would cover the people's unrighteousness. Through generations and generations of oppressive rule, God's people looked for the King

sent from heaven. Then, one silent night in Bethlehem, this King came. Jesus, the Eternal Son of God, took on flesh and was birthed into the world. Giving up His divine privileges, Jesus took on humility. Still, many came to bow before Him, presenting gifts to this King born in a manger.

Jesus is the King of kings who came to serve and live righteously on our behalf and for the glory of God. We were exiles, oppressed in captivity to sin. We were bound to deceit, lust, and pride. Displaced from our home, which was peace with God, we were sufferers in a fallen world, experiencing death, illness, and shame. Jesus paid our debts, cleansed us from sin, and forgave us. When we believe in His saving work, He gives us a heart of integrity so that we can love, fear, and worship God. We are no longer exiled from God. We no longer live our own destructive way. We no longer walk through grief and suffering without hope. In Jesus, God reclaims us as His own and exchanges our ruined clothing for Jesus's perfection. We are granted peace in our relationship with Him and are called back to our eternal home. Now belonging to Christ's kingdom, we are still exiles in this earthly world. Though we are children of God, we wrestle with hardship, setbacks, and trauma from sin. So we look to Jesus's second coming when He will bring His final kingdom, fully liberate us from evil, and give us complete joy in God's presence. Knowing this life is only temporary, we await the King who will wipe away the tears from our state of lament and heal our hearts from exile.

JESUS IS THE KING OF KINGS WHO CAME TO SERVE AND LIVE RIGHTEOUSLY ON OUR BEHALF AND FOR THE GLORY OF GOD.

IN WHAT WAYS DOES KING JEHOIACHIN'S PARDON IN 2 KINGS 25:27-30 SHOW HOPE
FOR GOD'S PEOPLE?

WHAT DOES JEREMIAH'S PROPHECY REVEAL ABOUT GOD'S CHARACTER?

WHEN DO YOU FEEL LOST, GRIEVED, OR ALONE? DURING THESE TIMES, HOW CAN YOU KEEP
YOUR PERSPECTIVE ON THE ETERNAL PROMISES OF GOD ACCOMPLISHED IN JESUS CHRIST?

Despite their sin, the Lord was working to restore His people from captivity and draw them back to the Promised Land.

READ EZRA 1, EZRA 3-4, HAGGAI 1-2

Return to Jerusalem

The kingdom of Persia replaced Babylon as the superior empire. King Cyrus of Persia saw the Lord's favor on the exiles and obeyed God's call to rebuild the temple in Jerusalem. Family leaders and priests traveled back to Jerusalem with the temple materials that Nebuchadnezzar had stolen during his invasion. Despite their sin, the Lord was working to restore His people from captivity and draw them back to the Promised Land.

Zerubbabel, a direct descendant of the Judean kings, led the project. He and other men began to build as the priests supervised. When they finished the foundation, some sang praises to the Lord for His goodness. But others, men of the older generation who had seen King Solomon's temple in all its majesty, were disappointed. These men wept for the glory days long gone. Now, as returned exiles, the mourners were more concerned with the appearance of the temple than what the temple represented. Glory would come from God alone and not the wealth of the city or its king. In their hearts, the men rejected the humble foundation Zerubbabel laid and thereby rejected the Lord's blessing.

The work was interrupted when enemies from the north came. As a result, the project was stopped. The people focused on constructing their own homes instead. But, Haggai, a prophet of the Lord, reminded them that they would not be fruitful in the land without the Lord. Zerubbabel heeded the Lord's command and began the work again. Meanwhile, by God's grace, permission was sent from Persia to continue. Through Haggai, the Lord encouraged Zerubbabel and assured him that His presence was near. Then, God said to him, "I will shake all the nations so that the treasures of all the nations will come, and I will fill this house with glory....The final glory of this house will be greater than the first....I will provide peace in this place" (Haggai 2:7-9). God told Zerubbabel the rule of all other nations will end, and God will reclaim His rightful possession of all things. The wealth reclaimed will reflect His honor and majesty. Even the most powerful kingdoms will be humbled and will come to worship God in His temple. The glory of this temple will be greater than the first one and will be a blessing to the faithful.

How would this temple come to pass? Zerubbabel was working among ruins, still under the hand of Persian authority. And, the sinful hearts of the people would defile the project and corrupt any temple offering to God (Haggai 2:11-14). The Judahites could not rebuild a holy temple, and a rebuilt temple could not keep the Judahites faithful. But, God Himself promised to bring down evil kingdoms, raise a holy dwelling place, and appoint a Zerubbabel-like leader who would be the exact image of God's glory and power. After generations of God's people longing, this holy temple descended from heaven. Such a temple was not made of brick or stone but of flesh and bone. Angels announced this temple's arrival. The sky shook, and the stars danced. Light shone from Bethlehem. Baby Jesus was born as the true temple and King.

Jesus is the fulfillment of the temple. John 1:14 states, "The Word became flesh and dwelt among us." The Word is Jesus, and He was eternally existing with the Father. The Son, equal in divinity, radiated the full glory of God. His first coming brought the very presence of God which was no longer kept behind temple walls. The Son took on flesh to reconcile us to God. His flesh was later crucified to pay for our sins. Jesus is also the true and better Zerubbabel who rebuilds God's kingdom. The saving work of Jesus conquers evil kingdoms and reclaims the earth as God's rightful possession. Ascended to the throne in heaven, Jesus reigns over God's kingdom with majesty and righteousness. When we believe in Him, Jesus establishes us as His holy nation and gives us faithful hearts. With the Spirit of God in us, we become temples of the Holy Spirit. Built up as God's Church, we radiate His light in the darkness. Though we are outwardly wasting away in this fallen world, we have a treasure in our hearts that is imperishable. Pressed on all sides, we draw near to God's presence through Jesus now and look forward to God's kingdom to come. When Christ returns, the New Jerusalem will descend from heaven. All other governments will pass away. The ruins of war, poverty, and crime will be turned into gold and precious jewels. This new creation will flourish and radiate the glory of God. This advent season, let us come to Jesus to dwell in and be strengthened by His marvelous light.

> THIS ADVENT SEASON, LET US COME TO JESUS TO DWELL IN AND BE STRENGTHENED BY HIS MARVELOUS LIGHT.

BEFORE THE BUILDING BEGAN, THE PEOPLE OFFERED SACRIFICES TO THE LORD AND CELEBRATED THE FESTIVAL OF SHELTERS, THE HOLY DAYS WHICH REMEMBERED GOD'S PRESENCE IN THE TABERNACLE. WHY ARE THESE ACTIONS SIGNIFICANT?

WHEN THE PROJECT WAS HALTED, THE PEOPLE'S EXCITEMENT ABOUT THE TEMPLE WANED, AND THEY BUILT HOMES FOR THEMSELVES. WHEN HAS DISAPPOINTMENT LED YOUR AFFECTIONS TO TURN AWAY FROM GOD AND TOWARD YOURSELF?

READ HEBREWS 12:26-29. HOW DO THESE VERSES GIVE YOU A FUTURE HOPE FOR GOD'S ETERNAL KINGDOM?

weekly reflection

SUMMARIZE THE MAIN PRINCIPLES YOU LEARNED.

WHAT DID YOU OBSERVE FROM THIS WEEK'S TEXT ABOUT GOD AND HIS CHARACTER?

WHAT DOES THIS WEEK'S PASSAGE REVEAL ABOUT THE CONDITION OF MANKIND AND YOURSELF?

HOW DO THESE PASSAGES POINT TO THE GOSPEL?

HOW SHOULD YOU RESPOND TO THESE PASSAGES? WHAT SPECIFIC
ACTION STEPS CAN YOU TAKE THIS WEEK TO APPLY THESE PASSAGES?

WRITE A PRAYER IN RESPONSE TO YOUR STUDY OF GOD'S WORD.
ADORE GOD FOR WHO HE IS, CONFESS SINS THAT HE REVEALED IN
YOUR OWN LIFE, ASK HIM TO EMPOWER YOU TO WALK IN OBEDIENCE,
AND PRAY FOR ANYONE WHO COMES TO MIND AS YOU STUDY.

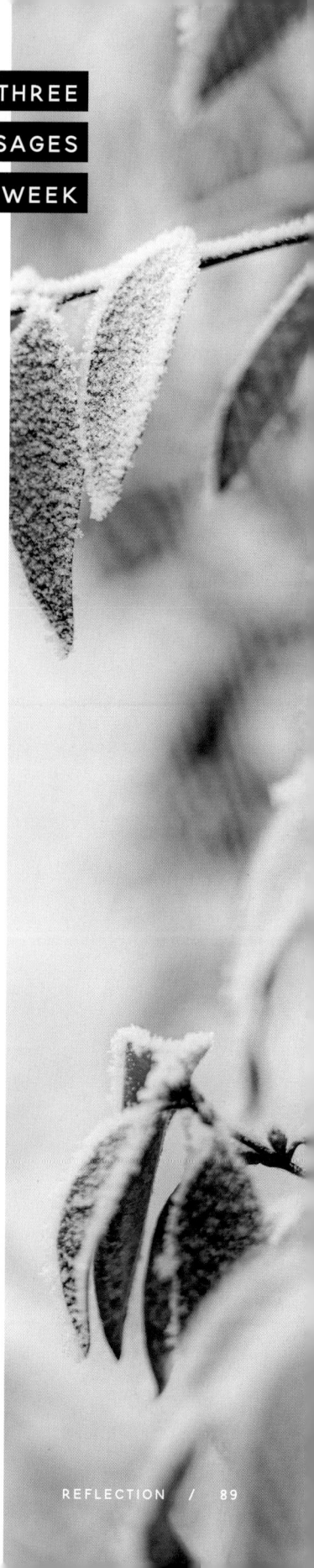

love
love
love
love
love
love

04 / 01
CANDLE LIGHTING DAY

love

THE FINAL ADVENT CANDLE REPRESENTS
GOD'S LOVE.

PRAYER

Lord, Your love is secure. When we seek to hide in our sin or when we forget Your tenderness toward us, we need only look to Christ to remember Your constant, enduring, and faithful love—a love exemplified in a little baby who left the splendor of heaven to live among sinners in the flesh, a love that laid down His life for His friends and who loved His enemies to the death, a love that sees all and knows all and endures all, a love that does not leave us to our desires but seeks our good with a never-ending and patient pursuit. Your love is all-satisfying. It is immeasurable and merciful, pulling us out of the darkness and making us blameless before Your throne through Christ's finished work on the cross. Oh how we love You, Jesus! Help us to love as You have loved us.

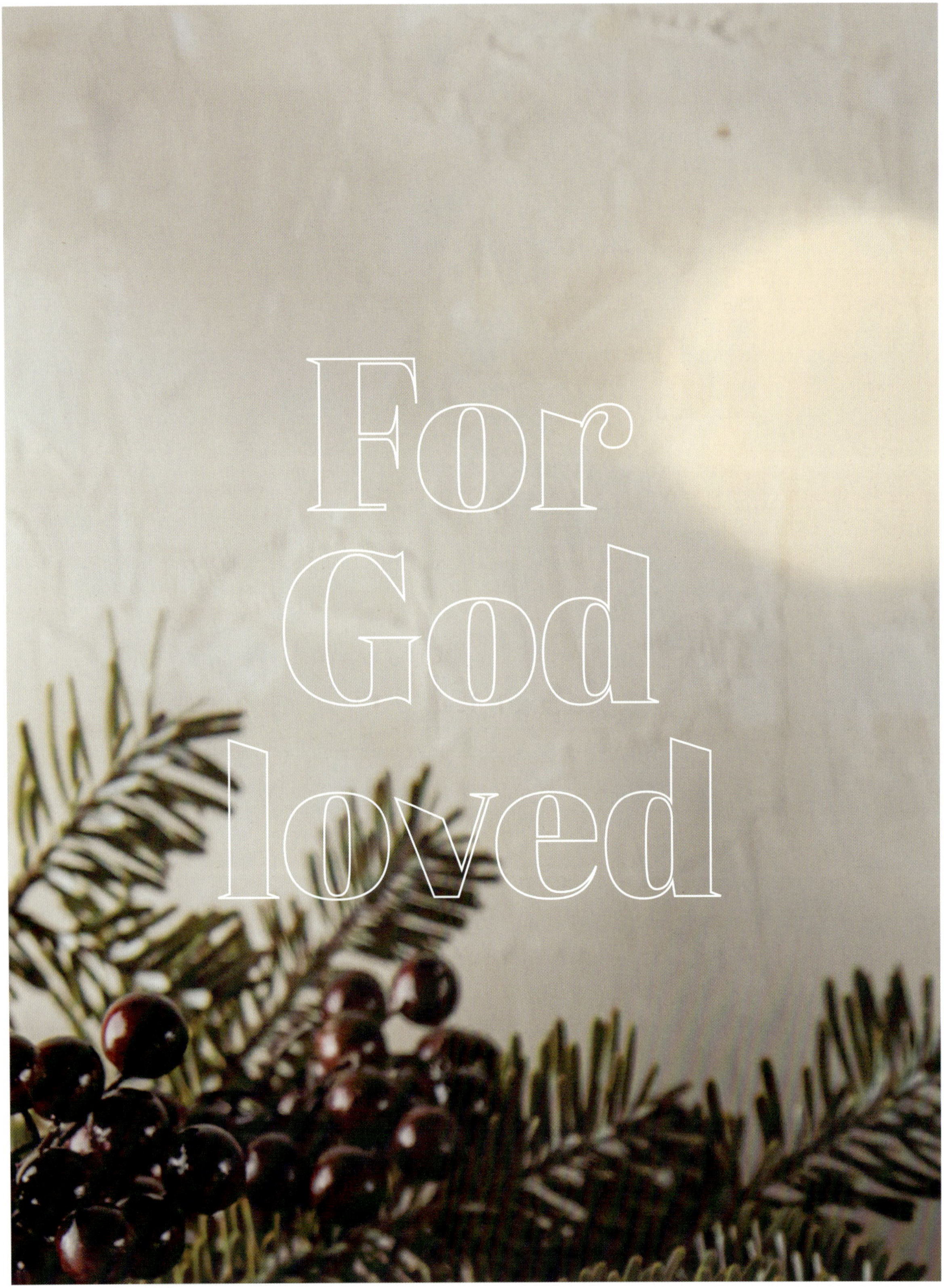
For
God
loved

For God loved the world in this way: He gave his one and only Son, so that everyone who believes in him will not perish but have eternal life. For God did not send his Son into the world to condemn the world, but to save the world through him.

JOHN 3:16-17

04 / 02

Raised up through the line of David, Joseph knew that the Messiah would come through his family.

Joseph

Genealogies served as a substantial record of the times, and in the opening chapter of the New Testament, we find evidence of generations and generations of God's faithfulness through each name listed. As we have worked our way through this list over the course of this study, we now come to the end with names famously appearing as the parents of Jesus Christ—Joseph and Mary. The conscious wording of the names speaks into the wonder and mystery of Jesus's birth, confirming the prophecy of a child descendent of Abraham, of David, and born to a virgin: "Jacob fathered Joseph the husband of Mary, who gave birth to Jesus who is called the Christ" (Matthew 1:16). Though Joseph was not the true, biological father of Jesus, God entrusted His one and only Son to him to raise and to father. Who is this man that he should receive such a righteous calling?

Joseph was the son of Jacob and the husband of Mary. However, Joseph was only engaged to be married at the time that Mary found out she was pregnant. Joseph knew this was not his child as they had obeyed the law that commanded sexual purity before marriage. This pregnancy was shocking, confusing, and possibly led to mistrust or doubt. We might have assumed some ways Joseph would have handled the news of his expecting fiancé, but his response tells us a great deal about his character. He was a righteous man and desired to obey and uphold the law, ultimately feeling it was necessary to end his engagement with Mary. However, he was also honorable and considerate, not wanting to publicly shame her, so he offered to do so secretly; a just and compassionate response to what seemed to be an unfair scenario for him.

Before he followed through with his intentions, an angel appeared to Joseph in a dream, exhorting him not to fear marrying Mary. The angel told him of the extraordinary things that were about to take place—that his betrothed was carrying the Promised One. Conceived by the Holy Spirit, this child was foretold by the prophets to save God's people from their sins and was to be named

Immanuel, meaning "God with us." Raised up through the line of David, Joseph knew that the Messiah would come through his family. There must have been overwhelming expectation and anticipation for the One who would fulfill that prophecy. We could guess there would have been sheer astonishment to follow this dream. Joseph may have had questions, and he may have even wondered why God would use him in this way. Yet, Scripture does not point us to his inquisition. Instead, it points us to his lack of hesitation, walking forward in faith and obedience, and he "did as the Lord's angel had commanded him" (Matthew 1:24). Joseph and Mary would soon become husband and wife, and they would travel to Bethlehem to give birth to their son, naming Him Jesus. Later taking his family to reside in Nazareth and working as a carpenter, Joseph, alongside Mary, would care for and raise Jesus and His siblings.

God the Father is Jesus's true Father and Mary His true mother, which exemplifies His humanity and divinity. But this does not leave Joseph as a random fill-in. Though Jesus was not born through the bloodline of Joseph but of Mary, there is still great importance and necessity to Joseph being His chosen earthly father. Brought forth from the line of Solomon and David, Joseph fell into the royal line. The heir to the throne had to come through the line of David to perfectly fulfill the prophecy. Mary, as Jesus's mother, established the bloodline connection, descending through the line of Nathan, David's son. But the legal right to the throne had to come through His father. Therefore, by adoption, Joseph provided Him the right to ascend the throne of David. In this way, Jesus fulfills the Davidic covenant which says, "Your house and kingdom will endure before me forever, and your throne will be established forever" (2 Samuel 7:16). And He establishes Himself in the way every king failed to do—as our one true King forever.

Those brought into the lineage of Jesus were included as part of God's grand orchestration of the redemption story. They did nothing to place themselves in such a story but were chosen by God purposefully and intentionally to bring hope into the world. We see it in every seemingly minor detail of their lives. He fulfilled every single aspect of the promise He gave, and He did so perfectly, using imperfect and ordinary people. The good news brought forth at Jesus's birth is good news for us today and forever. The God who paved a way for us from the very beginning has paved a way for us to be with Him for eternity by salvation through His Son. No matter who we are, where we come from, or what we have done, there is a place for every kind of person in God's redemptive story. May a recognition of this truth lead us to draw near and receive the hope of Jesus this season, and may it leave us in awe and worship of the One who sought us out and invites us in to this story of redemption.

THOSE BROUGHT INTO THE LINEAGE OF JESUS WERE INCLUDED AS PART OF GOD'S GRAND ORCHESTRATION OF THE REDEMPTION STORY.

WHAT DO WE LEARN ABOUT JOSEPH'S CHARACTER THROUGH HIS RESPONSE TO THE NEWS OF HIS SOON-TO-BE WIFE, MARY, BEING WITH CHILD?

HOW MIGHT YOU HAVE RESPONDED TO THE ANGEL APPEARING IN A DREAM, IF YOU, LIKE JOSEPH, HAD BEEN EXPECTING AND AWAITING THE MESSIAH TO COME THROUGH YOUR FAMILY LINE?

IN WHAT WAYS DO YOU SEE GOD'S INTRICATE AND PURPOSEFUL FULFILLMENT OF HIS PROMISE THROUGH THE LIFE OF JOSEPH? HOW DOES THIS LEAD YOU TO CONSIDER THE WAYS GOD IS USING THE SMALL DETAILS OF YOUR LIFE FOR A GRAND PURPOSE?

04 / 03

Mary shuddered at the angel's sight, but Gabriel told her not to be afraid, for God had found favor with her.

Mary, the Favored Woman

The disciple, Luke, began his account of Jesus's birth with a mention of the ruling king of Judea, King Herod. The Roman government designated Herod to rule over the Jewish people in Judea. At this point in redemptive history, subordinate to the powerful Roman Empire, God's people were still not free from authoritarian control. They looked for the Messiah, the Anointed One sent from heaven, who would be the chosen King over God's holy and just kingdom. As God declared in Genesis 3:15, this King would save God's people, reverse the curse of sin, and defeat all evil. By His power, the Messiah would bring down wicked authorities like King Herod. Until the Messiah's coming, the Jewish people suffered under Herod's violent reign and oppressive Roman taxes. These taxes led many to poverty. In this historical context, a young girl named Mary lived with her family in a meager town, Nazareth. But, in the impoverished conditions and darkness surrounding her, God saw Mary, favored her, and would choose her to execute His redemptive mission.

The angel, Gabriel, visited Mary in Nazareth. Mary shuddered at the angel's sight, but Gabriel told her not to be afraid, for God had found favor with her. Gabriel told Mary she would give birth to the Son of the Most High, the Messiah who would reign over God's people and restore the throne of David. Mary, young in faith, responded with innocent wonder and curiosity. She did not understand how she would conceive since she was a virgin and not yet married to Joseph. Gabriel gave Mary the sign of her cousin Elizabeth who was barren but now pregnant. Gabriel showed Mary that God, the Creator of the universe, has the power to create life within the lifeless. So, God could indeed knit together a son inside her womb. Mary heard and received the word that "nothing will be impossible with God" (Luke 1:37). Though she may have been fearful of others' accusations, she was full of faith and trust in God. By God's grace, she opened herself to the Lord's will and called herself His servant.

Mary quickly went to Elizabeth's home to witness this sign that Gabriel mentioned. Mary greeted her cousin, and in the womb, Elizabeth's son jumped for joy at the Messiah's presence. By the Holy Spirit's revelation, Elizabeth confirmed Mary was carrying the Anointed One. Elizabeth then stated, "Blessed is she who has believed that the Lord would fulfill what he has spoken to her!" (Luke 1:45). Because of her faith in the coming Messiah, Mary pleased God and would receive the covenant blessings of life and peace in God's presence. Her belief propelled her into a song of praise. She sang of the Lord's greatness and His salvation. Mary rejoiced in God's love and kindness toward her. Though the powerful and wealthy like King Herod lived in luxury around her, they were sinking in the darkness of their sin and separation from God. But Mary, a young and poor girl, thrived because she saw what God valued most. In her song, she highlighted the ethics of God's people: humility, fearing the Lord, and hunger for righteousness. Mary declared the supremacy of God's justice. She delighted in the victory of the Messiah growing within her, whose reign would topple the evil and the proud. Soon, Mary would encounter the pains of labor while holding onto the joy of seeing her Son. She embodied the longing and hope of advent, waiting with expectation for the Messiah's arrival.

Jesus was delivered into the world, but He is the true deliverer who births us into a new life with God. Those who are faithful are carried in Jesus, the Savior, and brought into the presence of God. We, like babies who are vulnerable and dependent, are susceptible to fall into our own sinful desires and are morally unable to please God on our own. But through faith in Jesus's saving work, we are covered in His righteousness and protected from the punishment of sin. Jesus is the Messiah who fulfilled God's covenant promises. He restored a people for Himself and established the kingdom of God. He defeated the rule of spiritual evil and humbled the prideful serpent. Though the evil and proud may still have power in this life, they do not have the final say. Jesus will return to judge and bring His eternal kingdom to earth. We must respond to the covenant promises accomplished in Jesus with humble faith like Mary. By the Holy Spirit, God will supply us with this faith we need. Let us remember the coming of the Messiah and have a servant heart bowed before His throne.

MARY DECLARED THE SUPREMACY OF GOD'S JUSTICE. SHE DELIGHTED IN THE VICTORY OF THE MESSIAH GROWING WITHIN HER, WHOSE REIGN WOULD TOPPLE THE EVIL AND THE PROUD.

HOW WAS MARY'S RESPONSE TO GABRIEL'S MESSAGE FROM GOD DIFFERENT FROM ZECHARIAH'S?

THE INCENSE ZECHARIAH OFFERED REPRESENTED THE PEOPLE'S PRAYERS FOR THE LORD'S SALVATION THROUGH THE COMING MESSIAH. HOW DID GOD INVOLVE ELIZABETH'S STORY IN ANSWERING THIS PRAYER? HOW DID GOD END HER SHAME THROUGH KEEPING HIS COVENANT PROMISES?

READ ROMANS 8:18-25. AT WHAT TIMES CAN YOU GROAN WITH GLADNESS THIS ADVENT SEASON?

The baby boy in the manger was God's Son — the fullness of deity embodied in human flesh who came to dwell with us.

God Dwells With Us

Jesus is here. From the immaculate conception to angels revealing the plan, and now to a decree which led Mary and Joseph to Bethlehem, the fulfillment of God's plan for a Messiah has come. So Mary found herself ready to give birth to this baby boy who had grown and developed within her. But as the story tells us, there was no room for her to give birth in any normal circumstances. Rather, the Son of God Himself came in a messy stable, full of animals and unpleasant smells. There, the baby boy rested in His mother's arms. But this was no ordinary child. The baby boy in the manger was God's Son—the fullness of deity embodied in human flesh who came to dwell with us.

In the very beginning, God desired to be with the people He had created. In Genesis 2 and 3, God dwelled with Adam and Eve. He lived among them, and they shared face to face fellowship. But that fellowship was broken when Adam and Eve chose to be their own god and disobey the words of the God who created and loved them. Though there would be consequences and pain born from that moment in time, God made a promise in Genesis 3 of one who would come and fix their sin. This One would restore fellowship between God and man.

Until that day, God was faithful to His people. He was faithful to be with them, though their sin would prevent intimate, face to face fellowship with the Holy God. In Exodus 29:45-46, God promised to be with His people. God said, "I will dwell among the Israelites and be their God. And they will know that I am the Lord their God, who brought them out of the land of Egypt, so that I might dwell among them. I am the Lord their God." God has always desired to dwell among His people. He led the Israelites in a pillar of cloud by day and a pillar of fire by night to be with His people. When the tabernacle was built, a cloud descended, and His glory filled the temple. God's presence was among them. Even then though, His presence was still separated from the people with a curtain into the holy of holies. Unfortunately, mankind's sin would keep God away because a holy God cannot dwell with sinful man. So as the story of Scripture unfolds, God's glory left the temple in Ezekiel 10. It did not come back. And God had not been physically present with His people since.

Until now. When Jesus came as a baby, His entrance into the world ended the absence of God's presence. All of the longing and waiting and hoping since the days of Adam and Eve had come to fruition. The longing for God to come near, face to face, in intimate fellowship once again was now a reality. And He came, not as a king or mighty warrior but as a baby. And as Matthew explains in this account, "all this took place to fulfill what was spoken by the Lord through the prophet." The God of all creation had planned since the beginning of time to send His Son, Immanuel, to be with His people and save the world. In Isaiah 7:14, the prophet spoke, "See, the virgin will conceive, have a son, and name him Immanuel." We remember that Immanuel means "God with us." When Mary gave birth to a son, this was no ordinary son. This was the very Son of God, fully God and fully human. This is God come as flesh. This is the moment all of Scripture had been pointing to since the time Adam and Eve sinned in the garden. The One who would come—He was now here. The time had come.

And this time God would not descend in a cloud and fill the temple, but God Himself would come in human flesh as a baby. Can you imagine, God, whose glory filled the temple, now lay His head in Mary's arms? Mary had never entered the Holy of Holies to be in God's presence; in fact, she could never have done that. But Mary held God incarnate. God had chosen to come into the world, free of temple walls and barriers, to dwell with man. His presence was with us.

This is what John's Gospel makes plain: "The Word became flesh and dwelt among us. We observed his glory, the glory as the one and only Son from the Father, full of grace and truth" (John 1:14). But that glory was revealed in the ordinary—in the mundane moments of life. Jesus nursed, transitioned to solid foods, learned to crawl and then walk, was potty trained, played with the neighborhood kids, endured puberty, and grew into a man.

While we do not often think about these mundane moments of glory, this is part of the beauty of Emmanuel. When God came to dwell with us, He became like His brothers in every respect (Hebrews 2:17) in order to redeem them in every respect, and that redemption secures an even greater dwelling-with-us—an eternal future when our broken world will give way to a new heaven and earth, when the dwelling place of God will forever be with man, and sorrows and sighs fly away. Emmanuel, God is with us. And because Emmanuel came, He will be with us—and we with Him—forevermore.

WHEN JESUS CAME AS A BABY, HIS ENTRANCE INTO THE WORLD ENDED THE ABSENCE OF GOD'S PRESENCE.

WHAT HAVE YOU LEARNED ABOUT GOD FROM THE WAY HE ORDAINED THE LINEAGE OF JESUS?

WHY IS IT IMPORTANT THAT GOD BECAME MAN?

IMMANUEL MEANS "GOD WITH US." READ MATTHEW 28:20. HOW DOES JESUS REAFFIRM THAT HE IS IMMANUEL IN THIS VERSE? WHY IS THIS SIGNIFICANT?

When we celebrate
the birth of Jesus each
December, we are
celebrating so much
more than His birth.

Christ the Savior is Born

The celebration of the baby born in Bethlehem is certainly a profound climax in the story of the Bible, but it is not the only high point. As we read the gospel narratives, we leave Bethlehem with the problems of sin and death still looming before us. We might take down our Christmas decorations after the holidays while still reflecting on Jesus's humble birth, but Bethlehem is only the beginning. The story of Mary and Joseph and the shepherds takes us down the path toward the most significant event in human history—the death of the baby born in Bethlehem. We are told in the first chapter of the New Testament why Jesus came: "he will save his people from their sins" (Matthew 1:21). He was born to save us. And because salvation was to be accomplished through Jesus's death, He was born to die.

Jesus's life on earth was not long—just 33 years. He was raised in a household with siblings and grew up as the son of a carpenter. Though we do not know much about Jesus's upbringing, we do know that He was aware of His purpose for coming, even at a young age (Luke 2:41-52). Though it is difficult for us to imagine, Jesus lived perfectly without sinning (2 Corinthians 5:21, Hebrews 4:15, 1 Peter 2:22, 1 John 3:5). From birth to death, He never gave in to temptation, never complained, never gave Himself to selfishness or lust or anger. His holiness was not merely an example to us. His holiness made Him uniquely qualified to fulfill God's purpose in saving us. Only the uncreated, sinless Son of God could reconcile sinful man to a holy God. He was the perfect, sacrificial Lamb who would take away the sins of the world (John 1:29).

Jesus was about thirty years old when He began traveling around Judea, teaching about God's kingdom. He called disciples to come with Him, and He taught them about who He was and the kingdom He was bringing into the world. For three years, He healed the sick, fed the hungry, rebuked the proud, touched the diseased, raised the dead, brought peace to the possessed, and preached salvation to all who would hear and even those who would not. He showed the world who God was and provided the only path to God the Father, for He Himself was God the Son. He lived the lowly and humble life of an itinerant preacher with no place to call home. He preached the good news of salvation through faith, fulfilling the Jewish law and causing much turmoil among the religious leaders who sought to quiet His claims of deity and His message of repentance and faith. They did not believe He was the Messiah. The more He preached about His mission to seek and save the lost, the more the religious leaders plotted against Him.

Jesus was no ordinary man. He was not merely a good teacher or a respected humanitarian. No, He was fully God while also fully man. He experienced the same temptations and sufferings that we do, and He endured faithfully until the end. He would not be deterred from His purpose to give His life as a ransom for those who would believe in Him for salvation. Jesus knew that the religious leaders plotted to kill Him, but He also knew that no one could take His life. He would give it willingly (John 10:18). God's plan to bring redemption to sinners was always going to be accomplished through the death of His Son. Jesus submitted Himself to the Father's plan and obeyed Him perfectly on earth.

During the Jewish celebration of Passover, a time of remembering God's deliverance of Israel from slavery in Egypt, Jesus was betrayed by one of His disciples and taken into custody by the Jewish religious leaders. He was mocked, stripped, beaten, and nailed to a crude Roman cross for claiming to be the Messiah. What those around Him did not realize is that He willingly walked the path from Bethlehem to the cross. The Messiah, the long-awaited hope of Israel, did not come to reign on an earthly throne. He did not come to upend Roman rule and free Israel from political oppression. He did not come to accumulate wealth or masses of followers. He came to die for sinners who needed deliverance from sin. He died on a cross outside the city of Jerusalem, giving up His life and bearing the weight of God's righteous wrath toward our sin upon His shoulders. He died in our place, paying the penalty of death for that sin (Romans 6:23).

But just as Jesus's story did not end in Bethlehem, His story does not end at the cross either. Three days later, God raised Him from the dead, proving that He accepted Jesus's sacrifice for our sins. Jesus had triumphed over sin, Satan, and death. The resurrection assures us that when we believe in Jesus for salvation, we, too, will be resurrected one day. We will enjoy life with Him forever in heaven where we will be free from sin, death, and despair. When we celebrate the birth of Jesus each December, we are celebrating so much more than His birth. We are celebrating His life, death, and life again, for it is through His death and resurrection that we find forgiveness of sins and eternal life. He accomplished the purpose the angel spoke of to Mary. He came to save His people from their sins! The story is still not over. After His resurrection, Jesus returned to heaven where He is seated at the right hand of the Father where He prays for us. One day He will return for us, and until that day, we live with hope for a glorious ending to the story.

WHAT WAS JESUS'S MAIN PURPOSE IN COMING TO US?

WHY DO YOU THINK THAT THE RELIGIOUS LEADERS WERE SO RESISTANT TO JESUS AND HIS MESSAGE?

HAVE YOU BELIEVED IN JESUS'S SACRIFICE FOR YOUR SINS? WHY OR WHY NOT?

Rejoice! Emmanuel has come to you. Rejoice! Surely He is coming soon.

The Second Advent

At last, Christmas day is here! For weeks the anticipation has been building to this one day when we celebrate that Christ the Savior is born for us. As you arrive at this long-awaited day, you may find yourself experiencing a variety of emotions. Excitement for the joy that the day brings or fear that perhaps December 25th will not bring you the happiness it promises. Perhaps you are filled with anticipation for time spent with those you love, or maybe it is a heightened sense of loneliness or anxiety over the interactions you would rather not have. Whatever your expectations for Christmas day, the reality is that the good news of great joy of Christmas is mingled with the sadness and suffering of a fallen world. Christmas day comes and goes, and we find ourselves still surrounded by conflict, sickness, sin, and death, and we may find ourselves wondering if Christmas was a reason to celebrate after all.

Rejoice, oh beloved ones! The story does not end here. As we anticipate Christmas morning, we are not only anticipating Jesus's birth but His return. During the Advent season, we allow our hearts to be stirred with longing for the birth of Jesus Christ so that we might long all the more for the day when He will come again. On that day, God will wipe away every tear from the eyes of those who have trusted in Jesus. On that day, the earth will be renewed, and our bodies will be glorified. On that day, the uninhibited presence of God will come down and dwell with His people. At last, there will be nothing to threaten our peace. Nevermore will our joy be mingled with sorrow. No more will our hearts be tempted to doubt the perfect love of God for us. On that day, our hope will find its final answer in Jesus.

Hallelujah! Christ has come, and He will come again. But how do we live in the in-between? How can we experience the hope, peace, joy, and love of Christmas in a still fallen world? We hold fast to Christ as we fix our eyes on eternity. If we are in Christ, His Spirit dwells in us. He is the one who gives us peace that surpasses understanding. He is the one who gives us hope to endure the trials of this life. It is His presence in us and with us that gives us true joy. He has made known to us the love of God, and we can experience it even now. We are strengthened by Him as we abide in His Word, and we are encouraged as we look ahead to what is coming. The first Advent calls us to a deep, expectant, Spirit-empowered, and joy-filled longing for the second advent.

The genealogy of Jesus is full of misfits and miscreants, the lowly and outsiders, all leading up to the One who would become lowly like us so that we could be exalted with Him. Now, the family tree of Jesus continues on with all who place their faith in Him. We are adopted as children of God and brothers and sisters of Jesus, and so we are heirs with Him in His kingdom. We can endure our present sufferings because of the joy set before us, knowing that even the most difficult or seemingly insignificant details of our lives are part of God's good plan to make us more like Jesus and bring us safely home.

Rejoice! Emmanuel has come to you. Rejoice! Surely He is coming soon. May our hearts swell with hope this Christmas and beyond as the words of Revelation 22:20 become our life's refrain: "Amen. Come, Lord Jesus."

DURING THE ADVENT SEASON, WE ALLOW OUR HEARTS TO BE STIRRED WITH LONGING FOR THE BIRTH OF JESUS CHRIST SO THAT WE MIGHT LONG ALL THE MORE FOR THE DAY WHEN HE WILL COME AGAIN.

HOW HAS YOUR ANTICIPATION FOR CHRISTMAS DAY STIRRED YOUR LONGING
FOR CHRIST'S SECOND COMING?

HOW DOES THE FUTURE HOPE OF THE SECOND ADVENT STRENGTHEN YOU
AS YOU LIVE IN THE IN-BETWEEN?

WRITE A PRAYER OF GRATITUDE FOR THE COMING OF JESUS CHRIST.

weekly reflection

HOW IS YOUR EXPERIENCE READING THE GENEALOGY OF JESUS DIFFERENT NOW THAN IT WAS WHEN YOU READ IT AT THE BEGINNING OF THIS STUDY?

WHAT DID THE WAY GOD WORKED THROUGH THE PEOPLE IN THE GENEALOGY OF JESUS TEACH YOU ABOUT WHO HE IS AND WHAT HE IS LIKE?

WHAT DOES THIS STUDY REVEAL ABOUT THE CONDITION OF MANKIND AND YOURSELF?

AS YOU CLOSE YOUR STUDY, READ MATTHEW 1 AGAIN
BEFORE ANSWERING THE QUESTIONS BELOW.

HOW HAS YOUR UNDERSTANDING OF THE GOSPEL CHANGED OR
DEEPENED AFTER SEEING GOD'S WORK THROUGHOUT HISTORY
TO BRING ABOUT THE PROMISED MESSIAH?

HOW SHOULD YOU RESPOND TO THESE PASSAGES? WHAT SPECIFIC
ACTION STEPS CAN YOU TAKE AS YOU MOVE INTO THE NEW YEAR
TO APPLY WHAT YOU HAVE LEARNED?

WRITE A PRAYER IN RESPONSE TO YOUR STUDY OF GOD'S WORD. ADORE
GOD FOR WHO HE IS, CONFESS SINS THAT HE REVEALED IN YOUR OWN
LIFE, ASK HIM TO EMPOWER YOU TO WALK IN OBEDIENCE, AND PRAY
FOR ANYONE WHO COMES TO MIND AS YOU STUDY.

What is the Gospel?

THANK YOU FOR READING AND ENJOYING THIS STUDY WITH US! WE ARE ABUNDANTLY GRATEFUL FOR THE WORD OF GOD, THE INSTRUCTION WE GLEAN FROM IT, AND THE EVER-GROWING UNDERSTANDING ABOUT GOD'S CHARACTER FROM IT. WE ARE ALSO THANKFUL THAT SCRIPTURE CONTINUALLY POINTS TO ONE THING IN INNUMERABLE WAYS: THE GOSPEL.

We remember our brokenness when we read about the fall of Adam and Eve in the garden of Eden (Genesis 3), when sin entered into a perfect world and maimed it. We remember the necessity that something innocent must die to pay for our sin when we read about the atoning sacrifices in the Old Testament. We read that we have all sinned and fallen short of the glory of God (Romans 3:23) and that the penalty for our brokenness, the wages of our sin, is death (Romans 6:23). We all are in need of grace and mercy, but most importantly, we all need a Savior.

We consider the goodness of God when we realize that He did not plan to leave us in this dire state. We see His promise to buy us back from the clutches of sin and death in Genesis 3:15. And we see that promise accomplished with Jesus Christ on the cross. Jesus Christ knew no sin yet became sin so that we might become righteous through His sacrifice (2 Corinthians 5:21). Jesus was tempted in every way that we are and lived sinlessly. He was reviled yet still yielded Himself for our sake, that we may have life abundant in Him. Jesus lived the perfect life that we could not live and died the death that we deserved.

The gospel is profound yet simple. There are many mysteries in it that we can never exhaust this side of heaven, but there is still overwhelming weight to its implications in this life. The gospel is the telling of our sinfulness and God's goodness, and this gracious gift compels a response. We are saved by grace through faith, which means

that we rest with faith in the grace that Jesus Christ displayed on the cross (Ephesians 2:8-9). We cannot save ourselves from our brokenness or do any amount of good works to merit God's favor, but we can have faith that what Jesus accomplished in His death, burial, and resurrection was more than enough for our salvation and our eternal delight. When we accept God, we are commanded to die to our self and our sinful desires and live a life worthy of the calling we have received (Ephesians 4:1). The gospel compels us to be sanctified, and in so doing, we are conformed to the likeness of Christ Himself. This is hope. This is redemption. This is the gospel.

SCRIPTURE TO REFERENCE:

GENESIS 3:15

I will put hostility between you and the woman, and between your offspring and her offspring. He will strike your head, and you will strike his heel.

ROMANS 3:23

For all have sinned and fall short of the glory of God.

ROMANS 6:23

For the wages of sin is death, but the gift of God is eternal life in Christ Jesus our Lord.

2 CORINTHIANS 5:21

He made the one who did not know sin to be sin for us, so that in him we might become the righteousness of God.

EPHESIANS 2:8-9

For you are saved by grace through faith, and this is not from yourselves; it is God's gift — not from works, so that no one can boast.

EPHESIANS 4:1

Therefore I, the prisoner in the Lord, urge you to walk worthy of the calling you have received,

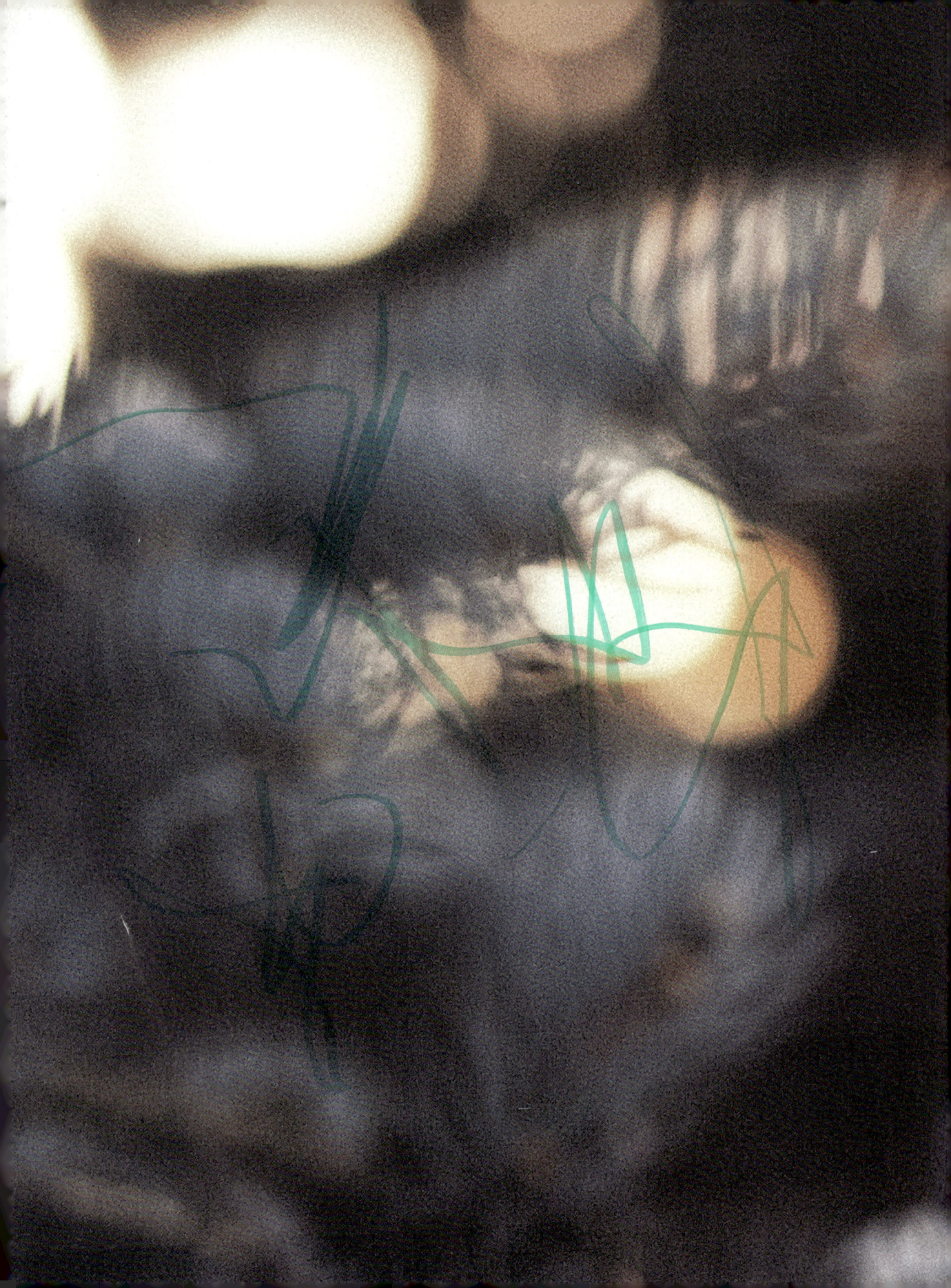